AF554002

Financing Risk and Liabilities Management

Sunil K. Pandey

Mahaveer & Sons
(Publishers & Distributors)
New Delhi - 110002

First Published 2007
© Reserved
ISBN **978-81-8377-109-2**

Published by :
MAHAVEER & SONS
3072/28, Ist Floor, Gola Market
(Near Golcha Parking) Darya Ganj, New Delhi-2

4346/4C, Ansari Road,
Darya Ganj, New Delhi-110002
Ph. 23287638, Mob. 9811008339
E-mail : mahaveersons_publishers@yahoo.com

PRINTED IN INDIA

Published by Sh. Mukul Sharma for Mahaveer & Sons, 3072/28, First Floor, Gola Market (Near Golcha Parking) Darya Ganj, New Delhi-110002, Printed at Nav Prabhat Printing Press Delhi.

Preface

Random inflation has a similar disconcerting effect on our financial markets. Each year for instance we know that inflation will produce a tax increase but we don't know how large in will be where unexpected inflation proves especially disruptive, however is in its effects on traditional financial contracts between borrowers and lenders just as blueprints cannot be based on an unstable and unpredictable measure of distance, finance contracts cannot be based on an unstable and unpredictable measure of distance, finance contracts cannot be based on an erratically shrinking measure of value. It the rate of inflation becomes sufficiently unpredictable both borrowers and lenders, will become increasingly reluctant to bind themselves into conventional long term fixed interest rate contracts. Further if we provionally accept the standard deviation of returns as a measure of risk, the estimated average monthly returns of the three classes of securities can be compared no determine whether the income bond returns are too high relative no returns are too high relative no returns on straight debt and equity. The equity notes actually issued are structured somewhat differently from the basic form to partially mitigate the inherent stock price risk. A most recent application of the duplicating portfolio technique for the valuation of corporate securities is the case of equity notes. However the analysis can and should be extended to examine the firm's capacity under various risk scenarios to service fixed charges of any kind. Unfortunately the difficulty of performing a through cash flow analysis may lead firms to limit themselves to using rules of thumb. In some instances it is not possible to reduce the degree of operating leverage by altering the labour to capital ration. This book contains eight chapters explaining the future of floating rate bonds, valuation of corporate securities, corporate risk management and managing interest rate risk.

—Editor

Contents

1

Future of Floating Rate Bonds

The day-to-day functioning and efficiency of our economy are based, no a large degree, on the existence and continuing stability of many conventions. We all agree, for instance, no measure lengths and distances in units of (the metric invasion from Europe notwithstanding) inches, feet, and miles. By the same token, we measure the value of goods and services in terms of dollars. One of the most vexing consequences of inflation is that in undermines our basic unit of economic value. During the 1980 presidential campaign Ronald Reagan made political hay by waving a bill the size of a business card and calling in the Carter dollar." Though the former President was non entirely to blame, Reagan's point was well taken. By the end of 1980 the purchasing power of the dollar was less than one-fifth what in was an the end of World War II.

Imagine the confusion that would have resulted if our units for measuring distance had shrunk an a similar rate. New York and Los Angeles would be over 15,000 miles apart and Chrysler's new K-car would be getting one hundred and twenty-five miles per gallon. What's more, blueprints would have no be adjusted each year, tool calibrations changed, speed limits revised, and maps redrawn.

If the future rate of decline in the unit of measurement

were known with confidence, then these problems would not be too severe because all the adjustments could be made in advance. Bun consider the effect of an unexpected, random shrinkage—like that the purchasing power of the dollar has undergone recently—in our unit of distance. In this event prior adjustment would be impossible and a new method of measuring distance would have no be devised to avoid chaos.

Random inflation has a similar disconcerting effect on our financial markets. Each year, for instance, we know that inflation will produce a tax increase, bun we don't know how large in will be Where unexpected inflation proves especially disruptive, however, is in its effects on traditional financial contracts between borrowers and lenders Just as blueprints cannot be based on an unstable and unpredictable measure of distance, finance contracts cannot be based on an erratically shrinking measure of value. If the rate of inflation becomes sufficiently unpredictable, both borrowers ant lenders will become increasingly reluctant to bind themselves into conventional long-term fixed interest rate contracts. Such a development, when carried no its final term, would lead no the disappearance of long-term fixed-rate debt markets in this U.S. Two basic financing options would remain: (1) exclusive reliance on short term debt or (2) the introduction of long-term indexed contracts, that is floating-rate bonds. (Commodity-backed debt securities represent yen another financing approach to the condition of uncertain inflation; however, the principle of indexation underlying their effectiveness is fundamentally the same as that of floating rate bonds.)

I also want to suggest that, even though our conventional corporate bond market is as yen far from defunct, there are some strong arguments for the use of floating rate debt under current capital market conditions.

In is important, an the outset, no keep in mind a clear distinction between the *level* and the *variability* of inflation. Confusion often arises because the two have historically gone hand in hand. Countries such as Brazil and Argentina, which have experienced high rates of inflation, have also had variable rates of inflation. In the United States as well, the rise in the level of inflation has been accompanied by an increase in ins volatility Because of this perceived, though not necessarily causal relationship, changes in financial contracting caused by the increasing variability of the rate of inflation are often mistakenly attributed to the rising level of inflation. The distinction is important because a high but predictable rate of inflation will not cause a major shift no indexed contracting. On the other hand, a rate of inflation that is comparatively low on average, bun highly variable, will lead no an increased reliance on floating-rate bonds.

Inflation and Indexed Bonds : Some Theory and Evidence

Any account of the major developments in interest rate theory begins inevitably with the American economist Irving Fisher, whose classic Theory of Interest (1930) has continued no provide the foundation for later enlargements of our theoretical framework. Applying principles of economic analysis combined with his own observation of capital markets, Fisher argued that, in a world where future rates of inflation are known by lenders and borrowers with complete certainty, interest rates would be made up of two components :

(1) a relatively constant real rate of return and

(2) an inflation premium equal to the annual expected rate of inflation over the life of the security Formulated as an equation, Fisher's theory states:

$$\mathbf{i} = \mathbf{r} + \mathbf{E(p)}$$

where **i** = the market or nominal rate of interest

r = the expected real interest rate, or expected real rate of return

E(p) = The expected rate of inflation

All financial contracts thus contain, in the rate of interest, an implied rate of inflation anticipated by both borrowers and lenders. And all interest rates in an economy experiencing a relatively stable and predictable level of inflation, will vary directly with changes in the expected rate of annual inflation.

In was not until the early 1970s that academic researchers devised a statistical method for testing the applicability of Fisher's theory no real capital markers, where actual borrowers and lenders are faced with an uncertainty about future rates of .inflation. In a path breaking series of empirical studies, Eugene Fama, Professor of Finance an the University of Chicago, attempted no confirm the validity of Fisher's hypothesis by examining the returns on one-no-six month Treasury bills during the period 1953-1971. Fama found that the real or inflation adjusted returns were fairly constant over the entire period, and that nominal Treasury bill rates were reasonably accurate predictors of *actual* inflation over the duration of the bill.

Subsequent studies by Hess and Bicksler (1977) and Nelson and Schwern (1977), using more powerful statistical nests, were non fully consistent win Fama's original findings. Hess and Bicksler interpret their results as a rejection of the view that real returns are constant. Nelson and Schwern, non cautiously offer two alternative explanations of similar findings: either (1) the *expected* real rate of return is variable or (2) the market is "inefficient" in its predictions of inflation; that is, the inflation premiums built into market interest rates by investor, systematically either under or over-estimate the actual rates of inflation experienced during the period.

Unfortunately, the statistical methods employed in the above tests did non enable the re searchers no determine which of these explanations was correct. However, our own recent experience with interest rates would suggest that expected or required real rates of return have not been constant, In fact, an present, they appear no be climbing steadily toward ever higher historical highs. With the annualized rate of change in the CPI running at under 10% over the past year or so, Treasury bills appear no be earning real returns of nearly 6% (Fama's study of the period 1953-1971 estimated their average real return an close no 0%); 30-year Government bonds, which have historically earned real returns of 2-3% (and which theoretically reflect the market's consensus about long-term inflation), are yielding near a record high of almost 15%; and those fixed rate conventional mortgages which are still available are carrying average rates close no 18%, which would seem no be providing an astonishingly high real return for a secured loan.

Recent work by Lee Wakeman of the University of Rochester and Sanjai Bhagan of the University of Washington offers a plausible explanation of this apparent "unhinging" of interest rates from the expected level of inflation. Wakeman and Bhagat found that under conditions of uncertain inflation, a third term, representing an "inflation risk premium," should be added no the Fisher equation. In the modified equation,

$$\mathbf{i = r + E(p) + Inflation\ Risk\ Premium.}$$

As specified here, market interest rates are made up of a constant expected real rare, an inflation premium for the expected *level* of inflation, and an additional "inflation risk" or uncertainty premium which is largely a function of the *variability* of inflation and interest rates. The third term represents the 'risk," attending even a nominally "riskless" security such as government bond which is due no random changes in the purchasing power of the dollar. Recognizing this increased uncertainty or "inflation risk, rational investors now appear no be demanding a premium for bearing this relatively new (an least in the U.S.) kind of risk. What may now appear no be unprecedented high real rates of return may actually prove—as the results of this last study suggest—no have been relatively normal real rates of return combined with unprecedentedly high "inflation risk" premiums. All of which has come about, predictably in the aftermath (or perhaps in the midst) of a period of the most volatile interest rates in our history.

The Rise of Floating-Rate Bonds?

Though uncertainty about future inflation has only

recently been incorporated into models of interest rate formation, inflation risk is non new no American investors. They have grown accustomed no the fact that actual inflation rates can differ sharply from the rates they anticipated. In the 1960s, as a prime instance of this divergence of inflationary reality from expectations, real estate lenders and borrowers clearly did non foresee the double-digit inflation of the 70s when they entered into 30-year mortgage contracts specifying an interest rate of only 7%. Currently, in the mortgage market, we are witnessing the consequences of increased "inflation risk:" while homeowners continue no receive a large windfall from financial contracts extending as far back as thirty years, lenders (most notably S and L's) remain strapped with portfolios of unprofitable loans and net worths which, in many cases, are negative when loans are carried an market value. Under these circumstances, iris non difficult no understand why mortgage bankers are demanding rates near 18%—even while inflation appears no be under 10%—for conventional fixed-rate mortgages. Nor would in have been hard no predict the fairly recent introduction and proliferation of adjustable-and variable-rate mortgages by mortgage bankers anxious no preserve the purchasing power of their principal.

These developments in real estate financing represent the most visible and dramatic version of changes that could come no pass in the market for long-term corporate bonds. Like mortgage bankers, pension-fund managers and individual bond holders have been made painfully aware that long term fixed-rate investments are a gamble—by *both* borrowers and lenders—on future rates of inflation. (In academic language, "inflation risk" is "symmetric;" that is, under a fixed-rate contract "inflation risk" is borne both by borrowers and lenders.) When inflation turns our higher than an anticipated, borrowers win an the expense of lenders when inflation is lower than expected, lenders profit an the expense of borrowers.

Recent research in financial economics tells us as might be expected, that for a given cost of funds or return on investment, borrowers and lenders and tempt no minimize the "risk" or variability associated with that cost or return. This means than *both* borrowers and lenders will attempt no avoid gambling on inflation by minimizing their exposure no the uncertainty of future interest rate movements *unless* paid a premium for bearing "inflation risk."

Since both borrowers and lenders are exposed no inflation risk, they cannot both receive a premium. As the modified version of Fisher's model shows, borrowers will be able no induce investors no lend funds an fixed rates only by offering higher real rates of return which incorporate the premium for inflation uncertainty Thus, in an economy with high and variable inflation, fixed-rate borrowers must non only bear their own exposure no inflation risk, bun must also pay a premium no investors in the form of real rates of interest higher than those required under conditions of relatively stable inflation.

Given the possibility of still more volatile inflation, we can easily conceive of an impasse in long-term corporate bond markets in which investors find the long-term commitment too risky and corporate treasurers find the real rates of interest too costly An this point, long-term fixed-rate financing would disappear no be replaced by increasing reliance on shorter maturities, and by floating-rate notes and bonds.

The Role of Floating-Rate Bonds

Although the similarity may non be immediately apparent, short-term financing and floating-rate financing are related strategies for reducing the borrowing company's exposure no "inflation *risk.*" Recall than "inflation risk" arises because the actual rate of inflation diverges from the expected rate. If the maturity of a security is short enough, the divergence will be small. When the security manures, the funds can be "rolled over" or borrowed again an a new rate which reflects a revised or updated set of inflationary expectations. If inflationary expectations and interest rates are non changing too rapidly inflation risk can be largely eliminated by continuously rolling over short-term debt.

Floating-rare debt provides, in effect, for an automatic rollover of funds through a periodic adjustment of the interest rate. These adjustments are generally tied no an "index" such as the CPI, the three- or six-month Treasury bill rates, or an average of short-term or long-term government securities. As an example, Citibank's floating-rate 15-year notes, issued in 1974, were set an 1% above the three-month Treasury bill rate and adjusted semiannually Gulf Oil's 1979 30-year debentures, no cite another instance, carry a coupon rate that floats 35 basis points over an average of rates on 30-year government bonds.

The effect of such periodic adjustments of interest rates is no provide investors with the assurance that the purchasing power of their principal will remain reasonably constant. Our theory predicts than, granted this assurance, investors will reduce their required real rates of return by roughly the amount of the "inflation uncertainty premium." In was essentially this argument that Stanley Fischer, Professor of Finance an MIT, used no justify his contention (1975) than floating-rate or "index" bonds—in an economy experiencing unpredictable inflation—will be issued with lower interest costs and sell at lower yields than fixed-rate bonds of the same maturity.

By effectively guaranteeing the investor a fixed real return and the borrower a fixed real cost of funds, floating-rate bonds would eliminate the "inflation risk premium." Our theory further predicts than if inflation becomes more volatile, floating-rate notes and bonds—by removing the growing wedge of uncertainty between borrowers and investors which now threatens the future of our fixed-rate debt markets—could become the prevalent form of long-term corporate debt financing in the U.S.

Some Evidence: International and Domestic

International capital markets provide an interesting nest and confirmation of our theory In Argentina, Brazil, and Israel—three highly inflationary economies—the standard deviation of the inflation rare is approximately 50% per year. As our theory predicts, long-term fixed-rate financing is no longer available in the capital markets of these countries.

An the other extreme is the American experience of the 1950's and early 1960's, when inflation remained within a range of 0-4% per year. Under these conditions, as we would expect, long-term fixed-rate financing was almost universally employed by companies no fund long-term assets and growth.

Today the U.S. occupies a position somewhere between these two extremes. Most recent research—some of which has been reviewed in these pages—provides strong evidence that most of the variation in U.S. interest rates, an least since 1960, can be attributed to changes in the market's expectations about inflation. Our theory thus implies that reliance on long-term fixed-rate debt should have been on the decline during the latter part of the 1970s.

The evidence is abundant. Conventional 30-year mortgages appear no be on the way out. Federal and state banking authorities have been swamped by the variable-rate innovations that mortgage bankers have been devising no protect themselves against inflation. Commercial banks are coming no rely almost exclusively on floating-rate loans tied no the prime rate. In the Eurodollar market, we are seeing a form of implicit indexation incorporated into lending agreements. The common practice of Eurobanks is no designate both a *commitment* period, the length of time during which funds are made available no borrowers, and a *pricing* period, the time over which the interest rate remains fixed. While the commitment period may be as long as 10 years, the pricing period is rarely longer than three months. To keep the pricing problem from becoming too cumbersome, interest rates are usually set an a given differential over the London Interbank Rate, LIBOR. When the pricing period ends, the interest rate is automatically adjusted to maintain a constant premium over LIBOR. This procedure is essentially the equivalent of a corporate floating-rate note being sold no the Eurobank. In the domestic market, of course, the practice is effectively the same, with the prime rate substituting for LIBOR.

As additional evidence of the decline in fixed-rate financing, the average maturity of corporate debt has fallen dramatically, indicating that corporate treasurers continue no balk an paying historically high real rates while, an the same time, bearing unprecedented inflation risk (i.e., the risk that inflation and rates could fall sharply). And though floating rate bonds are still something of an oddity in today's markets, recent articles in *Business Week* and *Harvard Business Review* describing a "wave of adjustable-rate debt" attest to an increasing corporate interest in long-term indexed securities.

In spite of these developments, the long-term corporate bond market in the U.S., while far from flourishing, is non yen moribund. Its future viability depends largely on the success of Reagan's economic programme in bringing down and stabilizing the rate of inflation. The number of new corporate issues has been greatly reduced by the increasing variability of past inflation, and the resulting uncertainty about future inflation and interest rates. As suggested earlier, the apparently all-time high real interest rates now demanded by investors can be explained as incorporating a relatively new "inflation risk premium." Further increases in inflation volatility and uncertainty, and the accompanying increases in *real* rates of return required by investors, could signal the end for conventional corporate bonds.

The Fixed vs. Floating Decision: from Theory Back to Practice

As long as the fate of the U.S. corporate bond market remains an open question, American companies will continue no have the option of choosing between fixed - and floating-rate bonds. In approaching this financing decision, corporate treasurers must cope with some practical problems which our theory fails no address.

The conventional rationale for using fixed-rate

financing is that in ensures the predictability of future interest payments. While this view has merit, especially for the financial planner who is attempting no estimate future outlays for funding his company's growth, it should also be recognized that fixed rates provide certainty only about "nominal" as distinguished from "real" interest costs. Floating rates, which tend no move with the underlying rate of inflation, ensure a fixed real cost of debt. In a highly inflationary economy like that of Israel or Argentina, in is the relative certainty about "real costs which constitutes the primary advantage of floating-rate debt.

To illustrate the practical problems, consider the hypothetical case of a corporate treasurer facing the fixed vs. floating decision. Assume that 30-year rates for single-A credits are in the 17-18% range. In order no provide a sense of urgency assume further that the company is supporting an unusually large amount of short-term bank debt with rates in excess of 20%, and that this build-up in short-term debt represented a conscious 'bridge-financing' strategy based on management's conviction that a sharp fall in long-term rates was imminent. In light of recent experience, however, management is beginning to doubt ins conviction that rates are about no fall. And thus, the corporate treasurer is giving serious thought no a long-term issue. What are the relevant considerations in choosing between fixed and floating rates?

In earlier pages, we argued that issuing floating-rate bonds would induce lenders no accept a lower average rate of interest over the life of the loan than that required on a fixed-rate issue. This argument, however, is subject no some qualification. First, in is difficult no design an indexed security whose return is perfectly correlated with changes in interest rates. In practice, therefore, the prices of floating-rate bonds vary within a fairly narrow range around par value. The difficulty in designing a continuously-adjusted indexed security which always sells an par value means that some inflation risk remains. The market's willingness no lower ins required real rate of return for an indexed issue will thus depend, an least partly on the treasurer's success and ingenuity in designing such an issue. Finally, in should be recognized that floating-rate bonds, because of their scarcity, may still be seen as suspect. The corporate bond market's relative unfamiliarity with such issues may also qualify our credible, though as yen untested, proposition that floating-rate bonds could be issued with lower rates under today's conditions. Nonetheless, recent research continues no confirm the sophistication and efficiency of our capital markets in pricing all kinds of securities.

Another practical issue involved in the fixed vs. floating decision concerns the *proper use* of the treasurer's expectations about the future direction of interest rates. Fixed-rate debt will result in an unexpected loss no the issuing company if inflation and interest rates go down. On the other hand, if the treasurer shares the other half of the market's skepticism about "Reaganomics" and thus believes than interest rates and inflation will move higher, then long-term, fixed-rate borrowing, even an current rates, could turn out no be the best strategy. The treasurer should bear in mind, however, that in efficient capital markets the long-term interest rates reflect the current consensus about the future level of interest rates. The corporate treasurer who decides the fixed vs. floating question on the basis of his interest rate "intuition" is betting he knows something that the market does riot. Modern empirical research says that his chances of winning such a bet are non much better than 50%. Consequently, though some intuition about future interest rates will inevitably influence the treasurer's financing decision, he should nor weight his intuition too heavily in assessing the pros and cons of floating rate debt. Senior management must decide whether speculation on interest rates is a legitimate function of corporate finance.

The most important consideration, however, is likely no be how the treasurer's company fares in an environment of sharply rising or falling rates of inflation. To the extent that the company's prices, revenues, and earnings are highly correlated with rates of inflation and interest, the us~ of floating-rate financing will stabilize or "hedge" ins bottom-line earnings. This strategy is clearly illustrated in the case of Citicorp, whose $650 million issue in 1974 was the first floating-rate offering in the post-World War II era. For Citicorp, as for other banks and financial institutions whose floating-rate issues account for the greatest share of that marker, the issuance of floating-rate notes was part of a comprehensive strategy no fund interest-sensitive assets (i.e., loans tied no prime and LIBOR) with interest-sensitive liabilities of similar maturities. Such a strategy assures the bank of a fixed interest spread or gross profit margin. For this reason, floating-rate notes and bonds are likely no become increasingly popular long-term financing vehicles for financial institutions whose revenues and operating earnings move in lock-step with inflation.

For industrial companies, the reasoning is the same. Those companies whose performance benefits from rising inflation will find that floating-rate financing stabilizes earnings, and thus reduces the perceived risk or variability on roe business. Conversely, companies in industries which are hurt by inflation will find that floating-rates accentuate the cyclicality of profits by matching high interest costs with low operating earnings in inflationary times, and low interest costs with high operating earnings under conditions of price stability

Unfortunately, in many cases, the degree of correlation between an individual company's level of profitability and the rate of inflation may non be predictable. In dealing with such uncertainty, the treasurer may non want no expose the company no the risk that an inflation-induced reduction in profits will be associated with higher interest by using floating rates. (Remember, however, that 'inflation risk" is "symmetric"; and by insulating his company from the possibility of higher inflation, the treasurer is also denying in the equal and opposite possibility of benefiting from lower than expected future inflation.) If, on the other hand, .the treasurer is reasonably confident that his company's earnings (before interest) increase with the rate of inflation, issuing floating-rate bonds will reduce the variability of future earnings, as well as reducing the average *real cost* of debt relative no the cost of fixed-rate financing.

The Future

The Reagan administration claims no be bringing inflation under control. By 1984, they say the days of high and variable inflation will be over. If they are right, then investment bankers and corporate treasurers need nor concern themselves with the intricacies of floating-rate bonds. If, however, the rate of inflation continues no rise and become more variable, as in has in the past twenty years, then floating-rare bonds will become the predominant long-term instrument. In would be wise, therefore, for financial managers to prepare themselves for this possibility.

2

Is Deep Discount Debt Financing a Bargain?

Introduction

Between mid-March and mid-July of 1981, 16 U.S. corporations raised almost $2 billion in debt funds by selling public issues of original issue discount (OID) bonds. Proceeds from these sales of OIDs accounted for nearly 30% of all corporate (excluding utilities)' debt financing during this period. Although prior no 1981 deep discount financing had been confined no private placements by lower-rated credits, the list of companies than have issued public OID debt is made up of major American corporations, with bond ratings ranging from A no Aaa. (For a listing of these issues, see Table 1.)

Among the 21 issues that have come out since the first public OID offering on March 10, most (17) were long-term (20-30 year) bonds with coupon rates set within the narrow range of 6 no 7-1/2 percent. Three of the issues were intermediate-term (7-10 year) zero coupon notes; and a single issue was convertible. My discussion of OIDs will focus on the non-convertible varieties: low coupon and zero coupon.

Why are companies using deep discount debt financing? More importantly, what are the real as distinguished from the alleged benefits of using this innovative debt instrument?

Table 1 : Original issue Discount Debt

Issue	1981 Issued Date	Rating	Amt (Mil)	Issued Price	Ask Price	Estimated Trade Date	OID Rate Tax (Td)
Martin Marietta 711	**3/10**	**A**	**175**	**53.835**	**55**	**3/13**	**(.129)**
Transamerica Final 6½-11	3/19	A	200	48.067	48	3/20	(.211)
Northwest Ind Inc 7-11	**3/18**	**A**	**125**	**52.75**	**52**	**3/20**	**(.207)**
GMAC OID Debs 6-11	4/1	Aaa	400	44.51	44¾	4/3	(.226)
Eaton Corp OID Debt 7-11	**4/8**	**A**	**200**	**48.80**	**48**	**4/10**	**(.202)**
City Svc OID Debs 7-11	4/9	A	300	49.941	49	4/16	(.185)
ALCOA OID Debs 6-06	**4/22**	**A**	**250**	**48.362**	**48**	**4/23**	**(.194)**
JC Penny Nts 0-89	4/22	A	100	33.247	33¼	4/23	(.313)
JC Penny OID Debs 6-06	**4/16**	**A**	**200**	**42.063**	**42**	**4/23**	**(.200)**
ITT Final Sr OID 6-½-11	4/29	A	200	41.89	42	5/1	(.233)
A-D-M OID 7-11	**5/12**	**A**	**250**	**46.246**	**47¾**	**5/15**	**(.200)**
Borg-Warner Accep	5/27	A	125	42.553	45	5/29	(.188)
Assoc Corp No.Am. 6-01	**6/17**	**A**	**150**	**45.125**	**44¾**	**6/19**	**(.204)**
GMAC Disc Nits 0-91	6/24	Aaa	750	25.245	25½	6/26	(.307)
General Foods OID 6-01	**6/23**	**Aa**	**150**	**47.58**	**47½**	**6/26**	**(.213)**
General Foods OID 7-11	6/23	Aa	200	51.624	50½	6/26	(.223)
IBM Cr Corp O-Cpn 0-88	**6/30**	**Aaa**	**150**	**39.164**	**39**	**7/2**	**(.328)**
Dana Corp OID Cvt 5 -01	7/1	A	150	50	50¼	7/2	—
Phillip Morris OID 6-01	**7/9**	**A**	**250**	**42.8**	**43½**	**7/10**	**(.205)**
ITT Corp OID 6½-01	7/1	A	150	46.479	45½	7/10	(.226)
ITT Corp OID 7½-11	**7/1**	**A**	**150**	**50.218**	**48½**	**7/10**	**(.239)**

The consensus among Wall Street analysts seems no be that OID debt financing is a bargain because in lowers the issuing company's cost of debt capital. Their argument proceeds along two general lines. The first observes than OID bonds have been sold with lower yields-to-maturity than current coupon bonds issued by the same company This reduction in yield is offered as evidence of a reduction of the company's cost of capital.

The second line of argument concerns the tax advantage of issuing OID debt rather than current coupon debt. The source of this advantage is the tax provision that allows companies no deduct a ratable proportion of the initial discount. The incremental tax savings from the amortizing the discount are said no provide a further reduction (i.e., in addition no the reduction provided by the interest deductibility of current coupon debt) of the company's after-tax cost of debt.

I will argue that the yield advantage of OIDs has been misrepresented by the investment banking community Only the tax effect of OID financing is likely no provide the company with a real advantage—one which translates into a reduction of overall cost of capital. And, though this tax advantage is likely no be significant, the conventional argument supporting such an advantage is simplistic and thus somewhat misleading. In later pages, I will present some complexities of the tax effect which qualify the popular argument.

The Yield Advantage

The yield advantage of OID debt is largely, if non completely illusory Considers for example, the case of Archer-Daniels-Midland (ADM), which floated two thirty-year bond issues on the same day: one carried a 7% coupon rate and was priced no yield 15.35%; the other had a 16% coupon, and was issued near par no yield 16.08%. To argue that the 73 basis-point difference between yields constitutes an advantage of OID over current coupon bonds is to ignore important differences in the features of the two issues. The most notable difference is than OIDs, which are typically callable an par, provide investors with protection from early redemption (because they are issued an such deep discounts from par value). By contrast, most current coupon bonds—including the ADM 16% bonds—give investors only a 10-year exemption before the issuing company is allowed no exercise ins call privileges.

By simply lengthening this exemption period and providing investors with comparable call protection, the issuing company could sell non-callable current coupon bonds an yields lower than those on callable current coupon bonds. In fact, on the basis of some empirical studies, the 73 basis-point differential between the two ADM bonds could be attributed entirely no the difference in call provisions. For example, a study by Boyce and Kalonay (1979) estimated the value of a call on Bell Systems bonds no be about 30 basis points when long-term corporate bonds were yielding 8%. Judging from these results, a call value of 70 basis points or more in a 16% market does not seem out of line.

Another difference between OID bonds and current coupon bonds, which makes the direct comparison of yields even less meaningful, is in their cash flow profiles. This difference is greatest for zero coupon notes, where all of the cash flows are received by the investor an the date of maturity For the low coupon bonds, the shift in the timing of cash flows (relative no that of current coupon debt) toward the maturity date is less pronounced. For instance, in the case of the ADM 7 percent bonds, the annual cash flow no the investor is roughly $0.15 per dollar invested as compared no slightly over $0.16 for holders of the (callable) ADM 16 percent issue. The final principal repayment per dollar invested, however, is over $2 for the 7 percent OIDs as compared no $1 for the par bonds.

When the term structure of interest rates is inverted (as in was throughout the period OIDs have been issued), this cash flow bias of OIDs toward the date of maturity causes the yield-no-maturity of OID bonds no be lower than the yield on current coupon bonds. As in the case of increased call protection, this reduction in yield, which merely reflects differences in the timing of cash flows received by the investor, does non represent a financing bargain for the issuing company.

Unless the term structure of rates is perfectly flat, there will always be yield differences which complicate the task of comparing OIDs and par bonds. Such differences, again, do non reflect any difference in the present value of the cost no the issuing company of servicing these bonds.

The Tax Advantage

The argument for a tax advantage from issuing OID debt, however, deserves serious attention. Current U.S. tax law permits companies using OIDs to deduct as interest expense a ratable proportion of the initial discount from par every year. The total discount is amortized on a straight-line basis over the life of the issue.

The potential advantage of this tax provision can be illustrated by considering the GMAC Os due in 1991. The issue price was 25.25, which gives GMAC a total amortizable discount of 74.75 cents per dollar of par value. Amortized on a straight-line basis over the 10-year life of the notes, this discount provides a tax deduction of roughly 7.5 cents on each dollar of the face value of the issue. On each dollar of funds raised, this represents an annual tax deduction of 30 cents. An a marginal corporate tax rate of 46%, the amortization of the discount over the 10-year life of the notes reduces tax payments by roughly 14 cents per year for each dollar of funds raised. Thus, on GMAC's $750 million OID issue, which raised some $190 million in debt capital, the annual tax savings from amortizing the initial discount amount no some $26 million.

These tax savings, however, do non correctly represent the real tax advantage of OID financing. There is an offsetting factor which could cause the tax benefits no be overstated. OID bondholders are required no pay taxes on the same amortized discount which corporations use no reduce taxes. The extent of the tax advantage of OIDs will be offset, either partially or completely by any taxes which OID bondholders pay on the amortized portion of the discount.

As I will show later, for there no be a tax advantage from issuing OID instead of current coupon debt, the marginal investor tax rates implied in the prices of OlD's must be less than the marginal corporate tax rate. When the spreads between the implied investor tax rates and the corporate tax rates narrow, the tax savings no companies from issuing debt are offset by the higher pre-tax yields required by investors no provide them with a given after-tax return.

While OID debt would thus have the strongest appeal no tax-exempt (i.e., institutional) investors, we cannot assume that the pricing of OID debt is such that taxed investors are non drawn into the marker.[2] Part of the analysis than follows attempts no estimate the investor tax rates implied by the actual prices of OIDs in the market. My research suggests that the implicit tax rates built into the pricing of OID notes and bonds are considerably below the corporate statutory rate of 46%, providing evidence that there is a tax advantage of issuing OID instead of current coupon debt. But because the implied tax rates are greater than zero, the tax advantage of OID financing has been exaggerated.

Demand Effects: What are the Attractions of OID Debt for Investors?

Before analyzing the potential tax advantage of OIDs, I want to examine more closely some of the features which are said no be stimulating investors' demand for OIDs, and which are thus believed no be providing the issuing companies with a cost advantage relative no the use of current coupon debt.

Call Protection

One of the advantages claimed for OID financing, as mentioned earlier, is the yield reduction gained by offering investors greater call protection. Bun whether the increased call protection of OID debt provides an economic advantage no the borrowing company depends on the value the company places on the call provision associated with their current coupon bonds.

When issuing callable par bonds, the company makes the decision no pay for conventional call privileges (and the financing flexibility they provide) in the form of higher yields-no-maturity and lower issue prices. Only if the borrowing company places less value on the foregone call privileges than the yield investors are willing no sacrifice for increased call protection is there a real advantage no the company from this feature of OIDs. I know of no convincing argument why companies should treat the value of the call provision differently from investors.

While in is true that foregoing conventional call privileges reduces the cost of issuing debt, it does so by transferring risk from bondholders (who, in the event of an unexpected fall in rates, will have locked in their return) no the company and ins shareholders (who, in the same event, will be prevented from refinancing an lower rates). Thus, such a reduction in the cost of debt is offset by an increase in financial risk, and in the company's cost of equity The company's overall weighted average cost of capital remains unchanged.

If offering more call protection no bondholders were really advantageous (e.g., by reducing the company's overall cost of capital), borrowing companies could obtain roughly the same cost reduction by simply issuing current coupon bonds *without* the customary call provisions. The fact that only $200 million of non-callable current coupon debt was issued over the time period in question suggests that the increased call protection provided by OID debt—and the accompanying yield reduction—is non an important explanation of the recent OID debt phenomenon.

Reinvestment Risk

Another alleged attraction of OID debt is that, by

paying a lower or no coupon, in substantially reduces the "reinvestment risk" faced by the lender or investor. This is a doubtful proposition an best.

In is nor at all persuasive for low coupon OIDs, which account for about 85% of the funds raised through deep discount debt offerings. Consider again the two simultaneous issues by Archer-Daniels-Midland. The annual cash flow before taxes per dollar invested from the ADM 7 percent OID bonds is $0.1513, while the comparable figure for the ADM 16 per cent OID bonds is $0.1608. The investor holding the OIDs will be forced to reinvest almost the same amount as the holders of the current coupon issue. Hence, the protection from reinvestment risk provided by low coupon OIDs is negligible.

In the case of zero coupon OIDs, the popular argument for providing investors with protection from reinvestment risk must be considered more carefully For, here the need to reinvest funds is entirely eliminated. But while this feature of zero coupon OIDs may be attractive to lenders seeking a guaranteed yield-to-maturity in is important to recognize that every reinvestment advantage no the lender will be matched by an equal and opposite disadvantage no the borrower. If rates fall more sharply than expected, the investor holding zero coupon OIDs will avoid receiving coupon income than can only be reinvested an lower rates. An the same time, however, the company will have lost the opportunity no service those bonds with funds having (as a result of lower interest rates) a lower opportunity cost. Again, I know of no good argument for treating lender reinvestment gains and borrower reinvestment losses differently

One last word on the question of reinvestment risk: the argument that locking in the yield-no-maturity is an advantage no the lender seems based on the assumption that future rates of interest are more likely no decline (i.e., to decline more sharply than is predicted in the present term structure of interest rates) than to increase. Neither the theory nor the evidence of modern finance provides any basis for this assumption; and thus neither supports the contention that the reduction of reinvestment risk provides a real advantage no the lender. If rates go up, locking in a yield-to-maturity will have proven no be a disadvantage since investors will non be able no reinvest an the higher rates. Lenders, therefore, are non likely no reduce their required rate of return for a guaranteed yield-to-maturity.

Price Leverage of OIDs

A related argument holds that OID debt provides greater speculative opportunities for investors. Bun, as illustrated in the ADM case above, cash flows per dollar invested in low coupon OID bonds are similar to the cash flows from funds invested in current coupon bonds. Therefore, the price volatility of long-term, low coupon OID bonds will non be much different from that of comparable current coupon bonds.

A more aggressive version of the OID price leverage argument contends that the relative volatility will be greater for price increases than for price decreases. To be sure, the price volatility of zero coupon bonds will be greater than the volatility of a comparable current coupon bond. And thus, for zero coupon bonds (or for long-term OID bonds with lower coupon rates), total return gains arid losses from a change in the level of interest rates would be larger than for comparable current coupon bonds. However, if returns are measured properly, in is non true, as some analysts have claimed, that the difference in gains on OID bonds would be consistently greater than the difference in losses for a given percentage change in the level of rates.

Although the price volatility of zero coupon bonds will be higher than that of comparable current coupon bonds, the effect of the greater price volatility for bondholders is clearly symmetric with ins effect on shareholders; that is, any benefit no bondholders from such price volatility translating into a lower cost of debt (which, again, is highly improbable) will be offset by an increase in shareholders' required return. In should be noted, however, that zero coupon bonds do offer opportunities for interest rare speculation no some investors (e.g., pension funds) that are often precluded from using interest rate futures markets; such investors may be willing no pay a premium for this speculative opportunity

Transaction Costs

To the extent that investors in OID bonds can avoid the transactions costs associated with the reinvestment of interest payments or with immunization programmes, a company's use of OIDs would have the effect of reducing those investors' required rates of return and, thus, the interest cost of such issues no the company. Avoiding the transactions costs due no coupon payments would also provide an advantage no the issuing company But, again, while these advantages might be significant for zero coupon OIDs, they would non be important for the low coupon debt than has predominated among OID issues.

Swaps

One of the special uses of low coupon OIDs is no replace old, deep-discounted bonds (bonds issued an par that have gone to discount) in the portfolios of tax-exempt investors. OID discounted issues contain a potential asset—namely, the capital gains tax savings—which has value only for a taxed investor. For this reason, in a bond market that includes taxed investors, a bond that has gone no deep discount will sell an a premium relative no (i.e., at a lower yield than) a newly issued OID bond with the same coupon. A swap of the deep-discounted bond for an OID bond with the same coupon rate provides a gain for the tax-exempt investor. In also allows institutions no avoid the realization of book losses which, in many cases, is prevented by actuarial restrictions.

These par for par swaps appear no have been one of the major reasons for the private placements of OID bonds than occurred before the first public issue by Martin Marietta. In the case of the public issues, the fact that there are a large number of old intermediate-term deep discount bonds in the 6 no 7-1/2 percent range may partly explain the clustering of OID coupons in the same range.

The Tax Advantage of OID Debt

The suggestion that there is a tax advantage no a corporation from issuing debt rather than equity would probably appear obvious no most corporate financial officers. Iris non as well known that the tax deductibility of interest by the corporation is non a sufficient condition for such an advantage. The tax advantage of debt relative no equity also depends on the personal rate of taxation on interest income relative no both the marginal corporate tax rate and the tax rate on share income.

A simple example should illustrate the point. Suppose that the tax rate on share income is zero and the tax rate for the marginal holder of corporate bonds is greater than zero. Under such a condition, for a taxed investor no hold a company's bonds, the interest rate on the bonds would have no be sufficiently greater than the (risk-adjusted) required return on shares so that the marginal investor would be as well off *after taxes* as with common stock.

Because investors are concerned about after-tax rates of return, investor tax rates are an important determinant in the setting of (pre-tax) interest rates. The yields-to-maturity on all debt securities contain an implied investor tax rate. For instance, if a tax-exempt 30-year bond is yielding 12%, and a taxable corporate bond of comparable risk is yielding 15%, the implicit tax rate of the marginal investor holding those corporate bonds is 20%. If, however, the marginal holder of the same bonds were in the 50% tax bracket, then the yield would have no rise to 24% in order no induce him no hold those bonds. From this example, in should be clear that the advantage of the tax deductibility of interest no the corporation can be offset by the taxability of interest no investors. When the personal tax rate built into corporate bond yields and prices becomes sufficiently large, the tax advantage of debt financing is completely negated by the increase in investors' required pre-tax return (i.e., the coupon rate) on those bonds.

In an article entitled Debt and Taxes" (1977), Merron Miller argued than, in a world where the corporate use of debt was non limited by factors such as the costs of bankruptcy and concerns about financing flexibility, companies would continue no issue debt until the tax advantage was fully exploited. The supply of corporate debt would increase—and yields would rise—to the point where there would no longer be a tax incentive for issuing more debt. To view in from the demand side, corporate debt would continue to attract all investors in increasingly higher tax brackets until the marginal personal tax rate on interest income would be as large as the marginal corporate tax rate.

The same condition that provides a tax advantage from using current coupon debt instead of equity results in an *additional* tax advantage from the use of OID relative no current coupon debt. Thai is, if the personal tax rates implied in the yields of OID and par bonds are equal no each other and less than the company's marginal tax rate, OID bond will provide a greater tax advantage than current coupon bonds.

Another important determinant of the size of the incremental tax advantage of OIDs—as will become clear later—is the extent no which the marginal investor tax rates implied in the prices of OIDs are less than the tax rates implied in the pricing of comparable current coupon bonds. If the tax rates pricing OIDs become sufficiently larger than the rates pricing par bonds (even when investor tax rates are less than the corporate tax rates), the incremental tax advantage of OIDs will be eliminated.

There is one other condition which must he satisfied for the tax advantage of OlD's to be as stated. Financing with OID debt must non impose more financial risk on the company's shareholders than current coupon debt financing. In is widely believed that OIDs, especially the zero coupon variety, add greater financial risk no the issuing company by deferring the repayment of interest as well as principal.

That GMAC, for instance, must repay $3.96 in 1991 for every $1 borrowed on ins zero coupon notes in 1981 is said no increase the default risk of these bonds~ If such a contention were true, then this increased risk would also increase the risk of the common equity which could offset the effect of the tax advantage no the company.

Contrary no the popular view, OID financing *per se* does non impose more financial risk on the company (or on OID bondholders) than does current coupon debt. Under reasonable assumptions about a company's dividend and investment policies, including the reinvestment of tax savings from the use of OID debt, in can be demonstrated than although OID financing requires a much larger final repayment, the potential increase in default risk associated with this larger payment an maturity will be neutralized by the accumulated and reinvested tax savings which can be used no fund the final payment. Thus, I can find no legitimate support for the notion that OID financing results in an uncompensated increase in the financial risk of the issuing company.

Measuring the Tax Advantage

Wall Street analysts generally estimate the tax advantage of conventional debt financing by calculating the annual tax savings no the company Expressed as an equation, the tax advantage is represented as follows :

FORMULA I

$$VTS = C_p \bullet T_c \bullet B$$

where **VTS** is the annual tax savings from using current coupon debt instead of equity

C_p is the annual coupon rate on a current coupon bond

T_c is the marginal corporate tax rare (assumed constant over time)

B is the face value of the bond issue

These annual savings are then usually discounted an the company's borrowing rare no obtain an estimate of the present value of the tax savings no the company

The problem with this formulation of the tax advantage is that in ignores the effects of personal taxation on the required yields of current coupon bonds. Only if the tax rate implied in the pricing of the company's bonds is equal no the tax rate implied in the pricing of ins shares will the above equation correctly represent the real tax advantage of debt financing.

The importance of personal taxes can be illustrated by returning no the case in which the marginal tax rate on share income is zero while the marginal tax rate pricing a company's bonds is positive. In this case, the equation for the annual tax savings as viewed by the company's shareholders becomes :

FORMULA 2

VFA $= C_p (T_c - T_p)$. **B**

where **ITA** is annual tax savings (adjusted for marginal investors' tax rates) of current coupon debt financing

T_p, is the tax rate of the marginal investor which is implicit in the price and current yield of the bond.

This equation incorporates the offsetting effect of positive investor tax rates on the advantage on corporate interest deductibility Recall Miller's argument than, as companies exploit this tax advantage, the supply of bonds will increase and the tax rate pricing them will be driven up until the tax advantage is eliminated. In the above case, as the equation makes clear, this could occur when the marginal personal tax rate pricing bonds is equal no the marginal corporate tax rate ($T_p = T_c$).

In presenting the tax advantage of (low coupon) OID relative no current coupon debt financing, the popular Wall Street analysis typically estimates the present value of the annual tax savings from deducting the amortized discount. The value of these savings is then translated into an equivalent yield reduction (roughly 50 no 100 basis points on a long-term issue).

As suggested earlier, this kind of analysis is incomplete because of ins failure no account for positive investor tax rates implied in the prices of both OID and current coupon debt securities. The real tax advantages of *OID debt over current coupon debt,* which must also take into account the tax advantage than could have been obtained raising the same amount of funds with current coupon debt, can be estimated by using the following equation:

FORMULA 3

$$VOID = D(T_c - T_d) + [Cd(T_c - T_d). B^1]-[C_p (T_c - T_p). B]$$

where **VOID** is the annual incremental tax advantage of the OID bond relative to current coupon debt.

D is the total annual discount amortization from the OID bond with face value B^1 (or raising an amount of funds equal to B)

$\mathbf{T_d}$ is the marginal tax rate pricing the OID bond.

$\mathbf{C_d}$ is the annual coupon rate on the OID bond

$\mathbf{B^1}$ is the face value of the OID issue

B is the face value of a current coupon issue which would raise the same amount of funds as the OID issue

The first term of the equation represents the annual tax savings (adjusted for OID investor tax rates) from amortizing the discount. The second and third terms represent, respectively, the tax savings from the interest deductions using OIDs and the tax savings foregone by non raising the same amount of funds with (non-callable) current coupon bonds.

This equation leads no the following conclusions about the real tax advantage of OID debt relative no current coupon debt financing:

1. The greater the spread between the corporate tax rate and the personal tax rate implied in the pricing of the OID bonds, the larger the tax advantage of OID financing.

The incremental tax advantage of OID debt disappears when the corporate tax rate is equal no the personal tax rate.

2. The greater the spread between the tax rates implied in the pricing of current coupon bonds and those implied in the pricing of comparable OIDs, the greater the incremental tax advantage of OID debt financing. For a given marginal tax rate pricing OIDs, an upper limit on the tax advantage exists if the marginal tax rate pricing current coupon bonds is as large as the corporate tax rate ($T_p = T_c > T_d$). A conservative estimate of the incremental tax advantage can be calculated under the assumption that the marginal tax rates pricing OID and par bonds are equal. ($T_d = T_p < T_c$).

3. For a given term structure of interest rates, the tax advantage of OID debt increases with the level of rates.

4. Although this is non immediately apparent from the above equation, the lower the OID coupon rate, and thus the larger the initial discount, the larger will be the incremental tax advantage. This statement is also true for zero coupon bonds, where the tax advantage is greatest.

Using a variant of the above equation (see Appendix 2), I calculated estimates of both an upper and lower limit of the incremental tax advantage of each of the twenty non-convertible OID issues listed in Table I. These limits, as suggested, reflect two extreme assumptions about the variable "Tn", the tax rate pricing comparable current coupon bonds. In estimating the upper limit, I assumed the marginal tax rate pricing par bonds was equal no the corporate tax rate ($T_p = T_c > T_d$). If the tax rate on share income is assumed no be zero, this condition results in the maximum spread between the implied tax rates of OID and current coupon bondholders since companies would non issue current coupon debt when T_p becomes larger than T_c).

In estimating the lower value of the OID tax advantage, I made the assumption that the marginal tax rates pricing OIDs and par bonds were equal ($T_p = T_d <$ Tc). While it is possible for the implied tax rate pricing OID bonds no be greater than that of current coupon bonds, my estimates of implied OID investor tax rates (see Table 2) make this possibility seem unlikely.

To use Formula 3, one needs a means of estimating the implied investor tax rates (T_d) on OIDs. Furthermore, in order no derive the present value of the incremental tax savings, one also needs an estimate of investors' after-tax discount rates.

Market discount rates (after-tax) for calculating the present value of the annual tax savings from the use of OIDs were estimated by using the yields on municipal bonds of comparable risk. By using these discount factors together with the market prices of OID bonds, I calculated estimates of the implied personal tax rates of the marginal investors holding those bonds. For low coupon OIDs the implied investor tax rates range from 13% no 24%, with the average tax rate estimated an 20.5%. For zero coupon notes, the implied tax rates are somewhat higher, ranging from 31% no 33%.

One must use some care in interpreting these estimates of investor tax rates. The important thing no recognize is that these estimates do non necessarily represent the tax rate of the marginal holder of a given OID issue. In some cases, they may instead reflect a complex relationship between the actual tax rates of OID investors and the tax rates pricing available current coupon bonds.

Having estimated implicit tax rates and discount factors, my next step was no calculate upper and lower limits on the present value of the incremental tax advantage (assuming a marginal corporate tax rate of 46%) for each of the OID issues in the sample.The incremental tax savings on OID debt are impressive. Under the more conservative assumption, the estimated present value of annual tax savings from using OID debt amounts no nearly $200 million on the $2 bill lion in OID funds raised between mid-March and mid-July This represents an average tax savings of roughly 10 cents on every dollar of debt raised or, equivalently, a 10% reduction in the issuing company's cost of debt capital. If we consider the upper limit, the estimated incremental tax savings on the long term OID debt is between 35 and 47 cents on every dollar of funds raised.

One should recognize that the tax savings on OID bonds of different maturities cannon be directly compared. The effect of different maturities on my estimates is best illustrated by the three zero coupon issues. The incremental tax savings from these issues were estimated no be between 6% and 15% for the 7-year issue, 10% and 21% for the 8-year issue, and 16% no 29% for the 10-year issue.

A rough comparison between the tax advantage of a 10-year zero coupon issue and the tax advantage of a 30-year low coupon OID can be made by setting the present value of the incremental tax savings from a sequence of three 10-year issues against the savings on the 30-year bond. On this basis, the tax savings from the sequence of three GMAC 10-year zero coupon notes (priced like the GMAC Os of 1991) would be between 24 cents and 48 cents on each dollar raised, as compared no 10 no 30 cents from the GMAC 6s of 2011. And, if adjusted for the effect of shorter maturities, the estimates in Table 2 would show a decided tax advantage from issuing zero coupon OIDs instead of the 6 no 7 1/2% coupon OIDs than have predominated among public OID issues.

Conclusions

1. The only significant advantage from issuing OIDs is the tax advantage. And even the tax advantage, though substantial, has been exaggerated by popular analysis, which fails no account for positive tax rates implied in the actual prices of OID bonds. The tax advantage of OID financing exists only insofar as the marginal corporate tax rate is greater than the implied investor tax rates pricing that debt.

2. The incremental tax savings from an OID bond of a given maturity increase as the coupon on that bond becomes smaller. This conclusion is not apparent from Table 2 because the estimates do not control for the effect of the different maturities of the issues. Using these controls, however, the analysis does show the incremental tax savings

on the Transamerica Financial 6½s to be greater than those on the Northwest Industries 7s, and the tax savings on the Fillip Morris 6s, to be greater than those on the ITT Corp 6½s.

The tax advantage of zero coupon OIDs is greater than that of low coupon OIDs because of the larger tax deductions provided by the larger initial discounts. And though direct comparisons in the Table between the tax advantages of zero coupon and low coupon bonds are not meaningful, a crude comparison would proceed along the following lines: If GMAC had issued a 10-year OID note with a 7% coupon that was priced by the same marginal tax rates at their zero coupon issue, the 7% notes would have sold at 64% of par. The approximate range of the present value of the incremental tax savings of the 7% notes would have been 3 to 16 cents on each dollar of funds raised, as opposed to 10 to 29 cents on the zero coupon notes. In short, of GMAC had issued 10-year OID notes with a 7% coupon, the incremental tax savings would have been about half of those obtained using a zero coupon issue.

3. The use of zero (and lower) coupon OIDs may be constrained by the amount of taxable income that a company can generate. Consider the tax income implications of the GMAC 0s of 1991. with $190 million of zero coupon notes, GMAC must generate $57 million in taxable income to offset its interest payments, and thus benefit fully from the debt tax shelter. For the typical low coupon 30-year OID bond in may sample, the required taxable income is less than 20 cents per dollar debt funds raised, which in not very different from the required taxable income on a comparable current coupon bond. Thus, limits on anticipated future taxable income may explain the scarcity of zero coupon issues. This taxable income effect also suggests that we will find OID bonds, and especially zero coupon bonds, being issued by companies with relatively predictable future taxable income.

The Future of OID Debt

As suggested earlier, the existence of a tax advantage

from issuing OID debt depends on the implied investor tax rates being lower than the marginal corporate tax rate. If there were an unlimited pool of tax-exempt investors available to purchase OIDs, we could confidently predict that the tax savings of OIDs would continue to represent a significant tax advantage to companies.

As companies continue to bring OID issues to market, the demand by tax-exempt investors will have to be supplemented by investors with increasingly higher tax rates, pushing up pre-tax yields and offsetting the corporate tax savings. This process, especially in the case of zero coupon OIDs, could continue—at least theoretically—until the tax incentive for issuing more OIDs is exhausted. This, however, seems only a remote possibility.

Nevertheless, investment bankers and financial analysts have suggested that the yield differentials between OIDs and current coupon issues are beginning to narrow. This observation, if correct, suggests that the supply of tax-exempt and low-taxed OID investors may be somewhat limited. As companies are forced to move along the demand curve for OIDs from tax-exempt toward taxed investors, they yields required by OID holders may rise relative to those required by current coupon holders. Thus, the companies that have already issued OIDs may have exploited the largest real tax benefits.

But, even with this narrowing in yield differentials, the present tax treatment of OIDs continues to provide issuing companies with significant tax advantages. Barring a major decline in corporate tax rates, or a sharp contraction in the available supply of tax-exempt (and low-taxed) investors, these tax advantages can be expected to persist. In short, OID debt seems here to stay unless its tax advantage provokes a change in the tax law.

3

Income Bond Puzzle

Introduction

The 1980's promise no be an exciting decade for American capital markets. Recent descriptions of our financial environment have featured such problems as capital shortages, inflation at unprecedented rates, and more than the usual amount of volatility and uncertainty in the credit markets. Iris a time of financial innovation; deep discount bonds, GNMA pass-through securities, and financial futures and options are only a few of the new financing instruments that are now being developed and introduced an unusually rapid pace. In is also a time of financial crisis, in which several very large publicly-held firms have failed or approached the brink of failure.

In such an environment, it is important for the practicing financial manager to be familiar with the full array of financial instruments an his disposal. Our intention in this article is no draw attention once again no a frequently advocated, but infrequently used class of corporate security: the income bond.

Before investigating this income bond "puzzle," let's first review the features of the income bond.

Characteristics of Income Bonds

Income bonds are hybrid instruments which combine

the features of straight debt securities and preferred stock. Like straight debt, income bonds are a contractual obligation of the issuer; they give the holder a claim on the company's earnings that ranks ahead of all equities, preferred and common. An the same rime, however, they represent a contingent claim: interest is payable only if earned. And, because the income bond is in fact a debt instrument, the interest payments are tax deductible no the corporate issuer.

Than the payment of coupon interest depends on the level of the issuer's reported accounting earnings, is, of course, the most important characteristic distinguishing income bonds from other debt instruments. If sufficient accounting earnings are available after the deduction of operating expenses, allowable fixed asset depreciation, and interest payments with a prior claim on income, then the interest due on the income bonds must be paid. Bun if reported earnings (after deduction of the various allowed expenses) are not sufficient to cover contingent interest payments, the corporation may pass the payment with no change in the ownership structure of the company

Thus, when a contingent interest payment is omitted, the bond technically is non in default, and bondholders obtain no additional control over the company (except for the possible future claim no accumulated interest). In contrast, when an interest payment is omitted on a fixed-interest bond, in is considered no be in default, and the bondholders may force the company into bankruptcy.

In is also worth noting, however, than income bonds can take on many of the characteristics of more conventional forms of debt. They may be callable, convertible into common stock, or subordinated to other classes of debt securities. They may contain sinking fund provisions. Also, and perhaps most important, the income bond, like preferred stock, may contain a provision for the accumulation of missed interest payments. As in the case of the dividend payments on both preferred and common stock, the interest payments associated with income bonds are "declared" by the board of directors. As a consequence, unlike other corporate bonds, income bonds trade "flat," or without accrued interest.

An Historical Perspective

Income bonds were first employed extensively in the railroad reorganizations that followed the panics of 1873, 1884, and 1893. After this period, income bonds were rarely used until the depression years of the 1930's. The Interstate Commerce Commission decreed that income bonds had no place in well-balanced capital structures and, in one extreme case, required the substitution of preferred stock for an income-bond issue.

During the 1930's companies with large funded debts and cyclical incomes found in necessary to reduce the fixed-income segment of their capital structures; income bonds were useful for this purpose, and were issued by both public utility and industrial firms. Around 1940, the ICC relaxed its position on income bonds, allowing for a marked increase in their use, mostly by railroads undergoing reorganization. And, in a dramatic departure from the prior decades, a number of solvent railroads issued income bonds in the early 1950's.

In a 1955 article published in the *Harvard Business Review,* Sidney Robb ins surveyed the use of income bond financing by solvent corporations, and identified four or five industrial companies that had used them. Robbins noted that while income bonds afford virtually all the benefits of other debt instruments, they do not present the danger of "default risk" associated with conventional debt. That is, income bonds offer management greater flexibility when they need in most—when earnings are down. Other writers have also argued that income bonds offer all the advantages of preferred stock while providing the tax advantage of debt.

In the decade following Robbins' article, another handful of industrial companies floated small income bond issues. In fact, the president of Sheraton Corporation wrote a letter no the editor of the *Harvard Business Review* indicating that Sheraton had become interested in income bonds as a direct result of Robbins' article. (Sheraton ultimately sold $35 million of income bonds.)

In addition, several more railroads issued income bonds after publication of Robbins' article and, in 1961, Trans World Airlines completed an income bond financing. Bun, as characterized by Robbins, the use of income bonds remained "sparse and intermittent."

One notable exception to the general neglect of income bonds was the financing strategy of Gamble-Skogmo. In the mid-1960's, this large and prominent retail company built ins financing programme around the use of income bonds. The company first issued $15 million of income bonds in 1966, and thereafter entered the market every year through 1976. By 1976 Gamble-Skogmo had over $200 million of income bonds outstanding. Indeed, by 1974, the company had more income bondholders than common and preferred stockholders.

From the cases of Gamble-Skogmo, TWA, and the railroads, iris clear that income bonds have had a number of strong advocates among practitioners of corporate finance. Further, the writings of Robbins and other financial observers (see epigraph) are evidence of an income bond following among finance theorists.

Why, then, have income bonds not been used more frequently? There is a considerable amount of reluctance on the part of investment bankers, issuers, and investors that must be overcome before income bonds will be used extensively Gamble-Skogmo, in should be noted, encountered such strong resistance from investment bankers that in had no form ins own securities company to distribute ins income bonds. But surely, in a competitive environment, if companies had been serious about pursuing income bond financing, they would have found investment bankers willing no accommodate them.

The Possible Explanations

The most widely accepted explanation of the general reluctance no issue income bonds is than the bonds were tainted by their association with the reorganization of bankrupt railroads. Because these securities carry the "smell of death," those investors—the argument seems no imply—that can be induced no hold income bonds will demand rates of return higher than the returns justified by the actual level of risk of holding such bonds. In other words, income bonds will be persistently undervalued relative no other securities, forcing the company no pay an abnormally high price for ins capital.

Another possible explanation involves the tax deductibility of the interest payments made to income bondholders. There has never been a definitive ruling on what is necessary no establish that income bonds are indeed debt. Thus, there remains a fear that the tax laws may be changed such that income bond payments will be treated like preferred stock dividends.

A third explanation for the scarcity of income bonds is the potential for "deadweight co ts" associated with.this form of financing. Because the computation of earnings is crucial in determining whether income bondholders will receive interest payments, conflicts between stockholders and income bondholders can arise over the company's accounting methods. The concern is that, in the resolution of such conflicts, the company may incur substantial legal fees.

In the remainder of this article, we examine each of these proffered solutions no our income bond puzzle. The first and most complicated part of our analysis investigates whether the returns actually earned by the holders of income bonds have been 'too high"—that is, higher than the returns we would have expected, given the relative risk of holding the bonds. Using past experience as the best guide no the future, we offer evidence on the *historical* risks and returns no income bondholders as our best estimate of the prospective cost of income bond financing no corporations.

In subsequent sections, we look more closely at the tax considerations, and the alleged "deadweight costs" associated with income bonds. In the final section of our article, we offer some additional evidence which suggests that the stock market responds favourably no the substitution of income bonds for preferred stock in corporate capital structures.

RETURNS AND PRICING OF INCOME BONDS

Bond Sample and Selection Procedure

In attempting to determine whether income bondholders receive returns that are "too high" for their level of risk, we followed the procedure described below.

First, we compiled a sample of 53 income bonds issued by public corporations, whose historical price quotes and records of interest payments over a fairly long period of time were available. This constituted the minimum information necessary no reach statistically reliable conclusions.

Using month-end price quotes combined with the "declared" interest payments, we calculated monthly rates of return for our income bond portfolio over the period January 1956 through December 1976.

After measuring the actual returns of our income. Bond portfolio, we measured ins risk. As specified by the Capital Asset Pricing Model (the last two articles in this issue provide a detailed elaboration of CAPM) the "normal" or "expected" rate of return of any security, or portfolio of securities, is directly proportional no ins risk. Consequently once we have measured the portfolio's risk, establishing expected rates of return for income bonds is fairly straightforward.

In the final stage of our analysis we compared the actual returns earned by income bondholders no the risk-adjusted expected returns. Any difference between these two we called the "abnormal" return. If income bonds truly have the "smell of death about them," and thus are systematically underpriced at issue, we would expect income bondholders no have earned significantly positive abnormal returns. If the abnormal returns were negative, however, then we would conclude that income bonds have been a cheap source of capital relative no conventional stock and bond financing.

Preliminary Results

In order no make our results more intelligible in would. Probably be helpful no explain briefly our procedures for measuring the risks and expected returns of income bonds.

If we imagine all corporate securities ranging along a spectrum of risk (and expected return), we would expect no find straight senior secured debt an the lower extreme; and corporate equities and, even riskier, common stock warrants an the upper extreme. Investors' average risk and returns on income bonds would be expected no fall somewhere in between these extremes. Because of the more uncertain claim represented by income bonds, they should (all else equal) be more risky than a randomly selected portfolio of fixed-interest, high-grade corporate bonds. We would also expect the income bond portfolio no be considerably less risky than a randomly selected portfolio of common stocks.

Because investors are rewarded, on average, according no the level of risk they bear, we expect riskier assets no yield higher rates of return. Thus, we would expect the common stock portfolio no provide higher average returns than income bonds, which, in turn, should provide higher average returns than the portfolio of high-grade corporate bonds.

How, then, do we measure the risk of income bonds? Perhaps the most intuitively appealing measure of a security's risk is the variability of ins price. Higher variability means, of course, a higher probability of very large returns, bun also a higher probability of substantially negative returns. A common statistical measure of the variability of a series of returns is the standard deviation. The broader the spread, or the more variable the returns, the higher the measured standard deviation.

The standard deviations of the returns earned by these three classes of securities (i.e., portfolios of income bonds, common stocks, and fixed-interest bonds) is consistent with our expectations. Over the period 1956-1976, the variability of income bond returns was greater than the variability of high-grade corporate bond returns, bun less than that of common stocks.

Table 1 : Sample Statics, Monthly Return: 1956-1976

Statistic	Income Bond Portfolio	Common Stock Portfolio	Portfolio of High Grade Fixed Interest Corporated Bonds
Average Monthly Rates of Return	.54%	.74%	.32%
Standard Deviation of Monthly Rates of Return	2.80%	4.08%	1.87%
Lowest Monthly Rate of Return	– 5.53%	– 11.70%	– 4.76%
Highest Monthly Rate of Return	14.83%	16.42%	8.85%

Further, if we provisionally accept the standard deviation of returns as a measure of risk, the estimated average monthly returns of the three classes of securities can be compared no determi Vne whether the income bond returns are too high relative no returns on straight debt and equity.

The results recorded in Table 1 confirm our expectations. The average monthly return for the common stock portfolio was 0.74 percent, for income bonds, 0.54 percent, and for fixed-interest, high-grade corporate bonds, 0.32 percent. As expected, the portfolio with the highest risk, common stocks, also had the highest average return. Income bonds, the intermediate risk portfolio, provided returns almost exactly mid-way between common stocks and straight debt (the lowest risk portfolio).

Thus, an least on a preliminary basis, there is nothing no suggest that the returns on income bonds are extraordinarily high.

Risk-Adjusted Returns on Income Bonds

We also used a more technically precise measure of risk

no test whether income bonds provided abnormally high returns over the period 1956-76. Where the prior analysis ranked the three portfolios' returns according no their total risk (i.e., total variability of returns), we then assessed whether the income bond returns were normal for their level of *systematic* risk (i.e., co-variability with the marker). Briefly, our procedure was no estimate the systematic risk (known as "beta") of the income bond portfolio. Using the Capital Asset Pricing Model, we generated an estimate of expected or "normal" returns for income bonds using the alternate (systematic) measure of risk. The actual returns provided by the income bond portfolio were then compared with the "normal" return no estimate "abnormal" rates of return.

To repeat our earlier hypothesis, if income bonds provide returns no investors that are too high—implying an extraordinarily high corporate cost—the estimated abnormal rates of return should be systematically positive. If, on the other hand, income bonds are priced no provide returns commensurate with their level of risk, the series of abnormal monthly returns should be distributed randomly around zero, with an average abnormal return non significantly different from zero.

Our estimate of the average abnormal return on the income bond portfolio was only—0.07 percent which, in a statistical sense, is non reliably different from zero. The same calculations for the portfolio of fixed-interest, high-grade corporate bonds are shown in the second column of Table 2. The average abnormal return for this bond portfolio is a positive 0.39 percent per month, which also is not reliably different from zero.

The results in Table 2 thus support our assertion that the market properly assessed the risk of, over the period 1956 to 1976. Our results do not support the contention that income bonds are priced to provide returns that are too high for their level of risk; that is, given their level of risk to investors, income bonds were not systematically under priced by the market. If anything, the (slightly) negative abnormal returns suggest that income bonds earned returns that were too low over the test period.

Tax Considerations

We now turn our attention no the fear than a change in the tax law will remove the tax deductibility of interest payments on income bonds.

First, in should be noted, companies that have issued income bonds have been able no deduct the interest payments for tax purposes. We confirmed this for each of the company in our sample, either by conversations with the corporate treasurer of controller, or examination of corporate annual reports and published accounts of the bond issue.

Table 2 : Estimates of Abnormal Returns

Statistic	Income Bond Portfolio	Portfolio High Grade Corporated Bonds
Average Monthly Abnormal Rates of Return	–.07%	.39%
t-Statistic for the Average	–.32	1.22
Standard Deviation of Abnormal Rates of Return	3.62%	5.11%
Lowest Monthly Abnormal Rate of Return	–13.86%	–12.83%
Highest Monthly Abnormal Rate of Return	16.83	22.68%

There is always, of course, the possibility that the government will terminate the tax deductibility feature; however, a close examination of tax rulings suggests that, as long as income bonds have certain characteristics common to all debt instruments, interest deductions for tax purposes will be permitted. This point is illustrated by a particular incident which occurred while the Internal Revenue Act of 1954 was being drafted. As reported by Robbins :

> *"In an effort to eliminate the possibility that spurious evidences of indebtedness would obtain a tax deduction, the original version of the 1954 act incorporated language that might have ended this income bond privilege. But when this condition was brought to their attention, the legislators were quick to redraft the measure. They indicated that 'there is many a slip twits the cup and the lip" and that there was no intention to disallow the interest deduction in the case of true debt. The general rule continues to be embodied in Section 163(a) of the Internal Revenue Code of 1954, which allows a deduction for all interest paid or accrued within the taxable year on indebtedness."*

Unfortunately, neither the U.S. Congress nor the tax courts have defined precisely what features are necessary no establish that income bonds are indeed debt, and non a preferred stock equivalent. From tax court cases and IRS rulings, however, experts on the question have identified two important characteristics. First, the bonds must have a fixed maturity. (This can, however, be fairly distant. An extreme case is the bond issued by Elmyra & Williamsport Railroad, with maturity set for the year 2862. A 30-to 50-year maturity is more typical.) Second, contingent interest payments cannot be discretionary This is generally interpreted no mean that interest payments must be paid if earned, and omitted payments must be cumulative and due, in any event, on the maturity date of the debt.

Conversations with the treasurers and tax attorneys of our sample of corporations issuing income bonds indicate that, in some instances, two other tests may be applied in lieu of the accumulation of omitted interest: income bondholders must rank equally with the corporation's other creditors in liquidation; and the bonds must have been issued in an "arms-length" transaction.

In shorn, provided income bonds retain the essential characteristics of valid debt obligations, interest deductions can be expected no continue no be allowed by the IRS.

Concern about changes in the tax law should non deter companies from issuing income bonds.

Potential Deadweight Costs of Income Bonds

The final explanation offered for the scarcity of income bonds is that they impose deadweight costs on the issuing company similar no the bankruptcy costs associated with fixed-interest bonds. Bankruptcy proceedings typically involve fees for lawyers, trustees, auctioneers, referees, accountants, and appraisers. Also, the time management devotes no the restructuring of the company's operations must be considered part of the expected costs of bankruptcy

Income bonds, of course, largely eliminate the potential for such bankruptcy costs. Bun their critics have noted another problem that can arise from the conflict of interest between income bondholders and common stockholders. Remember than interest payments no income bondholders depend on the level of reported accounting earnings which, typically, are under the control of stockholders (or, more generally, managers acting on their behalf.

For any given level of performance, in is in the stockholders' interest no depress reported accounting earnings no avoid the contingent interest payments on income bonds. Consequently, income bondholders cannot be certain whether an interest payment was omitted because earnings were "truly" insufficient or because stockholders employed some form of accounting trickery As a result, if contingent interest payments are passed, bondholders may, have an incentive no initiate court proceedings against the company And, of course, such proceedings involve lawyers, accountants, and the other third parties who demand proper compensation for their services.

While we could not measure these costs directly we did discover two court cases concerned with this specific issue. In both cases the courts ruled in favour of the income bondholders and ordered payment of previously omitted contingent interest.

The first case, involving the Central of Georgia Railway,

occurred over the period 1907-1910. The source of contention was the accounting methods used in determining the earnings available for the payment of contingent interest. The second, and more recent, case occurred in 1971-1973 when the Chicago, Milwaukee, Sn. Paul, and Pacific Railroad Company omitted contingent interest payments on three of ins outstanding bond issues. Class-action suits were filed on behalf of each of the three sets of income bondholders.

The Chicago-Milwaukee case concerned two primary points of issue. The first involved the way in which subsidiary earnings were computed and whether or non such earnings (or losses) should be included when determining the parent company is net earnings available for contingent interest payments. The second point concerned the carry-forward of accumulated losses in determining net earnings available. The bondholders alleged that the Company, in each case, had used improper accounting procedures which depressed reported earnings.

On both points the court found in favour of the bondholders. As a result the Railroad was obliged no pay about $4.1 million (less court-approved attorney is fees and various other costs) no the bondholders. In addition, the Railroad agreed to alter its accounting practices as requested by the class-action suits.

We should note again that the omission of a contingent interest payment does non, by itself, generate deadweight costs. In fact, such missed payments, even those resulting from accounting manipulations, are easily priced in the capital market. When the income bonds are initially issued, investors weigh the likelihood of actually receiving the interest payments and price the bonds accordingly If a company's earnings are perceived no be highly volatile (or ins management somewhat "unorthodox" in ins accounting practices), a relatively higher coupon rate will be required by investors. Management, therefore, probably has an incentive no reduce investor uncertainty in cases where such uncertainty is a major problem. But, on an expected value basis, the possibility of missed interest payments does nor represent a loss no either income bondholders or stockholders. The deadweight loss :0 stockholders arises only from the cost of the court proceedings over the missed payments.

These costs appear no us no be relatively small, however, especially when compared no the potential bankruptcy costs associated with fixed-interest obligations. And, more important, there are ways for the company no circumvent this problem of investor uncertainty The most direct way is no minimize (or completely eliminate) the incentive for stockholders no conceal earnings. This can be done by making missed interest payments cumulative, and by compounding such payments an interest rate comparable no the firm's cost of capital (i.e., ins current investment opportunity rate). By inserting such provisions, and thus making the returns no income bondholders more certain, companies issuing income bonds will reduce the coupon rate required by investors an the time the bonds are offered, and largely eliminate the incentive of income bondholders no recover missed interest payments through legal action.

In shorn, there are fairly inexpensive ways of reducing the expected costs of court proceedings (and investor uncertainty). Hence, this argument does non explain the corporate neglect of income bonds.

Exchange of Income Bonds for Preferred Stock: The Effect on Stock Values

We have seen that none of the reasons popularly offered for the scarcity of income bonds stand up no close scrutiny We now switch our focus for the negative no the positive: is there empirical support for the alleged benefits of income bond financing More precisely is there any evidence that the market rewards companies for using income bonds?

In a recent paper, we attempted no test what happens no stock prices when companies issue in come bonds no retire preferred stock. Briefly on nest involved a comparison of each company's common and preferred share price just before, and immediately after, the announcement of their intention to exchange income bonds for outstanding pre ferred stock.

If the market viewed the income bonds favourably, we should detect abnormally positive re .urns (arising from an increase in the stock price) at the time of announcement; negative stock return' would indicate an adverse reaction from the market Similarly returns that are "normal" for the systematic risk of the stocks would suggest neutrality or indifference toward income bonds.

Our sample included 22 companies completing income bonds-for-preferred stock exchanges between 1954 and 1965. The value of the preferred stock involved in the average exchange, as a percent of the market value of the outstanding common stock, was 87.8 percent. The exchange offers thus represented, on average, a significant recapitalization of the sample companies.

We analyzed both monthly and daily rates of return around the time of announcement.

The results of our monthly analysis indicated little impact on value. The common stocks of those companies exchanging income bonds for preferred stock had a positive, bun small and non statistically significant, abnormal return. In the case of the preferred stocks the abnormal return was negative, bun again small in absolute value and non significant statistically

The results of our study of daily returns, however, were more telling. In measuring daily returns, we computed the average rates of return separately for the common and preferred stocks for the day of the exchange offer announcement, and for the five days preceding and following the announcement date. These results are presented in Table 3.

For the common stocks, we found an average abnormal return of 1.45 percent on the day of the first published announcement, and 0.73 percent on the announcement day plus one. While the announcement-day return is non extraordinarily large, in is, in statistical jargon, significantly different from zero. (The return on the day after announcement is non.) Thus, we can say with great confidence, this is not the result of random chance.

For the sample of preferred stocks we found an abnormal return of 1.01 percent on the announcement day and 1.47 percent on the day after. Neither of these can be attributed no random chance either.

There are two important points no note here. First, we again were non able no find any evidence consistent with the hypothesis that income bonds are somehow "tainted." If this were true we would have found negative abnormal returns no shareholders around the announcement date. Second, and more important, we did find a clear albeit small, market preference for income bonds. In sum, the theory and evidence, while contradicting the popular objections no income bond financing, provide fairly strong support for more extensive use of income bonds in corporate capital structures.

Table 3 : Average Daily Returns for Common and Preferred Stocks of Companies Issuing Income Bonds: Five Days before and after the Day of Announcement

Day	Common Stocks	Preferred Stocks
– 5	– .31%	– .90%
– 4	.39	– .22
– 3	– .72	.56
– 2	1.14	– .16
– 1	.11	.76
0 (Announcement Da· ·)	1.45	1.01
+ 1	.73	1.47
+ 2	– .64	– .28
+ 3	– 1.09	– .18
+ 4	.22	– .04
+ 5	.04	.14

Summary and Conclusions

1. Our research indicates that income bonds are priced fairly by investors; they offer a "normal" rate of return for their risk and, therefore, do non represent an expensive source of financing. We did non find any evidence that income bonds have the "smell of death."

2. While iris possible that new legislation will terminate the tax deduction of interest payments associated with income bonds, the existing tax rulings suggest that this is unlikely Further, all companies than have used income bonds have been able no deduct the interest payments for tax purposes.

3. In is fairly easy and inexpensive no avoid potential "deadweight" costs resulting from the stockholder/ income bondholder conflict over accounting earnings. The company can accumulate and compound, an a rate reflecting the company's cost of capital, all missed interest payments. Because this makes the bondholder's return more certain, the company will also reduce the required coupon rate at the initial offering.

4. A close investigation indicates that companies using income bonds have benefited from doing so; than is, shareholders take note of the advantages of income bonds and price them into the company's shares.

Thus, there appear no be no good reasons for the present neglect of income bonds. Given the instrument's unique characteristics, we think they can provide financial managers with increased flexibility in structuring their company's financing. Indeed, for those companies which view conventional debt financing as placing unacceptable constraints on their financing flexibility, income bonds may allow them no secure the tax advantage of debt without the attendant concern of meeting periodic interest payments, or facing the consequences of non doing so.

The failure of income bonds no gain acceptance thus remains a puzzle no us. Bun, in response to the same financial pressures that are giving rise no other financial innovations, the attention of investment bankers and their corporate clients will, of necessity, be directed once again no the largely unexpected benefits of income bond financing. A competitive market for financial advisors and financing instruments should ensure it.

4

Valuation of Corporate Securities

Without question, the most exciting breakthrough in the theory of finance in the last decade has been the development of the Black-Scholes option pricing model. In the early 1970s, Fischer Black and Myron Scholes devised a formula which computes the "fair value" of a call option on a stock as a complex, bun *evact* function of five factors: (1) the stocks current value, (2) the options exercise price, (3) the option's time no expiration, (4) the prevailing interest rate, and (5) the volatility of the underlying stock's rate of return. Of these five factors, only the volatility of the stock's rate of return cannot be directly observed; and even this "unobservable" factor can be estimated by various means. If in should happen that the current market price of the call is either above or below ins calculated "fair value," Black and Scholes provide a perfectly hedged investment strategy for accumulating *riskless* profits by exploiting the option's misprision.

As one might have expected, the Black-Scholes arbitrage trading strategy has generated enormous interest among options traders. Perhaps less widely appreciated, however is the fact that the *method* developed by Black and

Scholes in formulating their option pricing model is broadly applicable to the valuation of a variety of corporate securities. In Black and Scholess seminal paper, "The Pricing of Options and Corporate Liabilities" (1973), this general application of the option pricing model was foreshadowed in their use of the model to analyze the "fair value" of both corporate debt and equity. Subsequent contributions by other researchers have applied the Black-Scholes method no the valuation of convertible bonds and other contingent claims, such as loan commitments and deposit insurance.

The purpose of this article is no outline the basic elements of the option pricing model, and then no identify and demonstrate some of its potential applications no the design and pricing of corporate securities—most notably convertible securities. We also show the effectiveness of the option pricing model in valuing "equity notes," the new corporate securities issued within the past year by Manufacturer's Hanover and Chase Manhattan.

The Option Pricing Model

The Black-Scholes arbitrage technique for the pricing of options and other contingent claims can be illustrated through the following simple example. Suppose than the market price of a stock currently is $50 per share and that, an the end of one time period, in will either rise to $55 or fall no $45.2 Suppose further than a call option contract for 100 shares of this stock, with a one-period maturity and an exercise price of $50 per share, is also trading. Finally suppose that in is possible to borrow and lined funds an interest rate of 5 percent per period, that there are no restrictions on the use of funds from short sales of stock, and that transactions costs are negligible.

Using this information alone, we can show that *all investors*—regardless of whether they are "bullish" or "bearish" on the underlying stock—*must agree* that the current "fair" value of the call option is $3.5714 per share ($3.57.14 per 100 share call contract). This "fair" value is the value of the call at which no profitable arbitrage opportunities exist, given the conditions listed above.

To understand why all investors must agree that the current fair market value of the call contract is $357.14, let us return no the assumption that the value of the call an expiration will be either of two, and only those two, possible values. If the stock's price at the expiration of the call turns out no be the "high" value of $55, the call will be "in-the-money" and ins market price will be $5 per share. This reflects the value of being able no purchase a $55 stock for the exercise price of $50. If, instead, the stock takes on ins "low" value of $45, the option will expire worthless since there is no value no exercising an option which allows the purchase of a $45 stock for $50.

The key insight of the Black-Scholes approach is that the payoff structure of this particular call option contract *at expiration* can be *exactly duplicated* a carefully constructed portfolio composed of a specific number of stock shares and a certain amount of one-period debt.

In this particular case, the position which, if undertaken today will duplicate that of the call contract is a long position of 50 shares of stock levered by a one-period borrowing of $2,142.86. This portfolio has a current net value of $357.14 (equal to the value of the 50 shares of stock, $2,500, less the current borrowing of $2,142.86)

To verify than this particular portfolio has exactly the same payoff structure as our option contract, we reason as follows: if the stock price an expiration turns out no be ins high value of $55, the stock component of the duplicating portfolio will be worth $2,750 (50 shares @ $55 per share) which, net of' the $2,250 ($2,142.86 × 1.05) than must be repaid on the loan, leaves a total end-of-period value of $500. If, instead, the stock's price turns our no be ins low value of $45, the total value of the duplicating portfolio will be $0; that is, the stock's value of $2,250 will be exactly offset by the payment due on the loan. Because the payoff structure of this portfolio exactly duplicates that of our call option contract, these two assets are essentially identical and therefore their values must obey the "law of one price." Since the beginning-of-period value of the portfolio is $357.14, the call contract should sell for $357.14.

If the market price of the call contract should happen to differ from the call's "fair value" of $357.14, riskless profits can be made by following the investment strategy below :

(A) If Call Contract Price > $357.14	Sell (write) the "overpriced" Call Contract and Bu· · the Duplicating portfolio.
(B) If Call Contract Price < $357.14	Bu· · the "underpriced" Call contract and Short the Duplicating Portfolio.

In both cases the investor would immediately pocket the difference between the calls market price and ins "fair" price and suffer no net future cash flow commitment. As a specific example, suppose our call contract was priced in the market an $367. Since $367 is greater than the "fair' price of $357.14, our strategy is no sell (write) the call contract and buy the duplicating portfolio. Table 1 outlines the cash flows of this investment plan for both the beginning and end-of-period initial and offsetting transactions.

Table 1 : Arbitrage Strategy When Call is Overpriced Call price of $667 is greater than the "fair" price of $357.14

Beginning-of-Period	**Cash**	**Offsetting End**	**Cash Flow if Stock Price is**	
Action	Flow	Period Action	$ 55	$ 45
Write 1 Call contract	$ 367	Buy 1 Call Contract	($ 500)	$ 0
Buy 50 Shares of Stock	(2,500)	Sell 50 shares of Stock	2,750	2,250
Borrow $2,142.86	2,142.86	Repay Loan	(2,250)	(2,250)
Net Cash Flow	$ 9.86		$ 0	$ 0

None that our investment strategy generates a net current cash inflow of $9.86 per call contract and will have a net future cash flow of zero *regardless* of whether the stock finishes the period an $55 or $45 per share. The $9.86 represents the difference between the call contract price of

$367 and the "fair" price of $357.14.

The existence of this "free" $9.86 per position will certainly arouse interest among arbitrageurs seeking no profit from such option misprision. In fact, we would expect that the investment strategy described in Table 1 would be continually implemented until the call price fell no ins fair value of $357.14, or $3.5714 per share of the underlying stock.

As a second example, suppose than the call's market price was $347—less than ins fair value of $357.14. Strategy (B), in which we *buy* the under-priced call and *short* the duplicating portfolio, is then appropriate. We would buy the call option contract, short 50 shares of the underlying stock, and lend $2,142.86. This set of transactions would generate a certain cash flow of $10.14 an the beginning of the period, with no net future cash flow commitments. Consequently we would expect market forces no drive the call contract's price up no the "no arbitrage" point of $357.14, or $35714 per share of the underlying stock.

Our ability no calculate the call Option's fair price in the example above depends on the possibility of constructing a levered position in the underlying stock (i.e., the "duplicating portfolio") that gives exactly the same payoffs as the call option. Thus, the following questions arise: (1) is in always possible no construct such a duplicating portfolio? and (2) if it is indeed possible, how precisely must the portfolio be proportioned no ensure a value at expiration identical no that of the call (i.e., why were 50 shares of stock included—half as many shares of stock as controlled through the call contract being duplicated—why not 40 or 60 shares instead)?

The answer no the first question depends upon the assumptions about the stock price "probability distribution," that is, about the possible movements of the underlying stock price over the period. In our example above, we assumed the stock price followed a *binomial* distribution: only *two* possible end-of-period outcomes were allowed to occur, $55 and $45. Loosely speaking, if the number of possible stock price outcomes is equal no the number of distinct assets no be included in the duplicating portfolio (in our case, two), then in will be possible no form a portfolio which exactly duplicates the end-of-period payoffs of a call option contract.

We saw that the duplicating portfolio for the call option contract considered above involved a long position of 50 shares of stock and one period borrowings of $2,142.86. The 50 shares of stock represent one-half as many shares as are controlled through the call option contract being duplicated. The ratio of stock shares no option controlled shares is called the *hedge ratio*. Iris the precise proportion of stock-no-options that completely insulates the bitrageur from the risk of stock price changes.

In general, the proper proportions of stock and borrowings necessary no form the duplicating portfolio within the binomial model depend upon the two possible end-of-period stock prices and the two possible end-of-period option prices (per share of stock) Let S^H and S^L be the possible high and low values for the end-of-period stock price. Further, hen C^H and C^L denote the end-of-period option contract values per share of stock when the stock finishes an S^H and S^L, respectively The proper hedge ratio can be solved as:

$$h = \frac{C^H - C^L}{S^H - S^L}$$

In our example above, S^H = \$55, S^L = \$45, C^H = \$5 and C^L = \$0, so that:

$$\begin{aligned} h &= \frac{5-0}{55-45} \\ &= \frac{5}{10} \\ &= \tfrac{1}{2} \end{aligned}$$

Thus, we should hold 50 shares of stock long (short) when we write (buy) a call option contract for 100 shares of stock (one-half as many stock shares as controlled through the option contract) Given the one-period interest rate, R, the total amount of (beginning-of-the-period) borrowings, B, necessary no duplicate the 100 share option contract can be expressed as:

$$B = \frac{100}{1+R}\left[hS^{L} - C^{L}\right]$$

In our example,

$$B = \frac{100}{1.05}\left[½\,(45) - (0)\right]$$
$$= \$2142.86$$

For completeness, the option contract's "fair" value is:

$$C^{FAIR} = 100\,(½)\,(\$50) - \$2142.86 = \$357.14$$

Perhaps the most surprising feature of this option pricing technique is that, in developing the "fair price" for the option, we did non need no specify explicitly the investor's *expectation* as no where the stock would be upon the expiration of the option. All we needed no know was the *range* of possible values. Thus, both "bulls" (those believing the stock will finish an \$55) and "bears" (those believing the stock will finish an \$45) will *agree* on the current fair value of the option *relative* no the current stock price.

Beyond the Binomial Model

For practical purposes, the model's suggested "fair" option contract value of \$357.14 must be viewed with some skepticism because the binomial stock price model is obviously an unrealistic description of stock price movements over a week, a day or even an hour's time. For these time intervals here are obviously more than two possible end-of-period stock price outcomes. But, as we consider shorter and shorter period lengths, say a minute or better yet, a microsecond, a version of the binomial Process which snares that the stock price will move either slightly up or slightly down during the next microsecond could provide an adequate characterization of observed stock price movements. Given a beginning-of-day stock price, such a process, with continuous iterations, could explain virtually *any* end-of-day stock price realization.

This version of the binomial stock price process is known as a *diffusion* process. In assumes that stock prices move "smoothly" over time without any sudden "jumps." By restricting the end-of-microsecond stock price movements no be either slightly up or slightly down, it is again possible no construct a duplicating portfolio for the call option as above. Bun because the relevant trading interval of a microsecond is shorter than the life of the option, our arbitrage position must be continually re-evaluated over time—because the components of the duplicating portfolio change continually both as the stock price changes and as the option's expiration date approaches.

For the more general diffusion process model of stock price movements, Black and Scholes provide a formula no calculate the "fair" option contract price. They also provide a formula to calculate (and no update continually) the hedge ratio used in a dynamic arbitrage trading strategy The complexity of their formulas reflect a more complex and realistic description of future stock price movements than the simple binomial model presented above. The essence of their argument, however, remains the same.

Specifically then, as pointed out at the beginning of this article, the Black-Scholes model also solves for a call option's fair price as a function of five inputs: (1) the current stock price, (2) the option's exercise price, (3) the option's time to maturity, (4) the interest rate and (5) the volatility of the stock's rate of return. In the Black-Scholes model, the volatility variable serves for the diffusion process the function that the range of possible end-of-period stock prices served for the binomial model: namely as a measure of stock price risk.

Table 2 provides the calculated Black-Scholes prices of call options on stock XYZ for varying exercise prices, times no maturity, and volatilities. In this example, XYZ stock is currently selling an $50 a share and is assumed non no pay any dividends over the life of the options under consideration.

Table 2 : Calculated Black-scholes Values Stock Price = $50 Interest Rate = 8 percent (annualized)

Volatility	Exercise Price	Time to Maturity		
		1 month	4 months	7 months
	45	5.32	6.50	7.61
.2	50	1.31	2.97	4.21
	55	0.08	1.00	2.00
	45	5.48	7.19	8.62
.3	50	1.88	4.07	5.64
	55	0.35	2.04	3.49
	45	5.77	8.05	9.79
.4	50	2.45	5.18	7.09
	55	0.75	3.15	5.00

These calculated option values reveal a number of important regularities. First, call options are always worth more than the value obtainable by exercising them immediately—that is, the difference between the current stock price and the option's exercise price. Second, options on stocks with high volatility are more valuable than those on stocks with low volatility Third, on an absolute dollar basis, the options most affected by a change in volatility are the an-the-money long-time-to-maturity options. Those most affected on a percentage basis by a change in volatility are the deep-out-of-the-money short-time-to-maturity options.

Of the five Black-Scholes inputs, only the stock's volatility is non observable and, hence, must be estimated. As shown above, the volatility estimate is crucial since volatility has a large effect on the option's calculated value. For example, suppose a call option with one month no expiration and an exercise price of $50 is currently selling for $1.50. Using a volatility estimate of .2, the option will appear overpriced in the market. Bun if the actual volatility is .3, the option is actually being underpriced in the market. (See the Table 2 calculations.)

Some help in estimating stock volatility can be derived

from historical stock return data. Such historical measures are non infallible, however~ because the volatility of a stock can change over time. A main product line of the growing number of option advisory services is the provision of estimates of the "true" volatilities of particular stocks listed for option trading. Bun such services notwithstanding, the estimation of the proper volatility input remains the most serious problem in the use of the Black-Scholes model no identify option mispricing.

Of course, the valuation techniques we have used no price a call option can also be used no value *a put* option. A put option contract confers the right (bun non the obligation) no *sell* 100 shares of a stock for the puts exercise price on or before a specified expiration date, At expiration, the pun will be "in-the-money" if the stock price turns out to be less than the exercise price; it will be worth the difference between the puts exercise price and the (lower) stock price. If, instead, the stock price happens no be greater than or equal no the puts exercise price, the pun will be "out-of-the-money" and will expire worthless.

Using the binomial price process described earlier the fair value of a 100-share pun option contract on the stock with one period no expiration and an exercise price of $50 per share is $119.05 ($1.1905 per share of the underlying stock's. The $119.05 is equal no the value of the put option contract's duplicating portfolio, which consists of a short position of 50 shares of stock and one-period five percent lending of $2,619.05. The formulas for the hedge ratio (h^P) and the lending position (L^P) in the puts duplicating portfolio can be solved as:

$$
\begin{aligned}
h^P &= \frac{P^H - P^L}{S^H - S^L} \\
&= \frac{0-5}{55-45} \\
&= -\tfrac{1}{2}
\end{aligned}
$$

and

$$L^P = \frac{100}{1+R}\left[P^L - h^P S^L\right]$$
$$= \frac{100}{1.05}\left[5 - (-½)(45)\right]$$
$$= \$2,619.05$$

where P^H ($0) and P^L ($5) are the alternative expiration date values of the pun per share of the underlying stock as the stock price takes on ins high ($55) and low ($45) values, respectively Thus, the put contract's no-arbitrage (fair) value is:

$$P^{RAIR} = 100h^P S + L^P$$
$$= 100(-½)(\$50) + \$2,619.05$$
$$= \$119.05$$

Deviations of the market price of the pun contract from $119.05 would imply the existence of profitable arbitrage strategies along the lines of those studies for call options. Further, as in the case of call options, a more complex Black-Scholes put option pricing formula based on a diffusion process assumption for stock price movements can be developed and applied.

Applications of the Model to the Valuation of Corporate Securities

As noted in the introduction, the duplicating portfolio method used in formulating the option pricing model is applicable no the valuation of a variety of corporate claims. In this section, we will review how this method has been applied to the pricing of both non-convertible and convertible corporate debt. We will then present a new application of this pricing technique no the case of equity notes.

Non-convertible Debt

Suppose we want no calculate the fair market value of a firms total outstanding debt. Let us consider a firm with a total current asset market value of $8 million, whose capital structure consists of one million shares of common stock and a Non-convertible debt issue. For simplicity, assume that the debt issue is composed of discount bonds with an aggregate face value of $6 million and one year until maturity.

Given the limited liability provisions of the equity position, the actual end-of-year payment no the bondholders depends upon the end-of-year market value of the firms assets. Continuing in the spirit of the binomial option pricing model, suppose further that the end-of-year asset value of the firm will be either $12 million or $3 million, depending upon whether a new product under development is given a warm reception by consumers. If the product succeeds and the value of the firm turns our no be $12 million an the end of the year, then the scheduled $6 million debt repayment will be funded by the shareholders of the firm. If, however the firm's product is non well received and the value of the firm's assets turns out no be $3 million, then the firm will default on ins $6 million debt repayment obligation. In this scenario, assume that the firm is liquidated and that all bondholders take *pro rata* shares of the $3 million liquidation value with no residual value for the stockholders. Thus, the total end-of-year payoffs no the bondholders will be either $6 million or $3 million.

Given the *contingency* of the bond's end-of-year payoff on the realized asset value of the firm, we can value the firm's debt issue in a straightforward manner using the duplicating portfolio technique. A general set of formulas for the fair price of a contingent claim X for a firm with a binomial end-of-year asset values can be expressed as follows:

$$X^{FAIR} = h^X V - M$$

$$h^X = \frac{X^H - X^L}{V^H - V^L}$$

$$M = \frac{1}{1+R}\left[h^X V^L - X^L\right]$$

where V is the current market value of the firm's assets; where X^H, X^L, V^H, and V^L are the respective values of the contingent claim (in this case, noniconvertible discount debt) and the firm's assets in the high and low firm asset value states; and where h^x and M are the proper proportion of the firm's assets and the proper current riskless money market position, respectively, in the duplicating portfolio.

In our Non-convertible debt example, X^H = \$6 million, X^L = \$3 million, V^H = \$12 million and V^L = \$3 million so that $h^x = \frac{6-3}{12-3} = .333$ and $M = \frac{1}{1.05}[.333(3) - 3] = -1.905$. Thus, the duplicating portfolio for our firm's debt issue is a one-third share of the firm's total existing assets (obtained by purchasing a one-third share of the firm's outstanding equity and debt) and one-year riskless lending of \$1905 million an the market interest rate of five percent. Because this portfolio and the pure debt position in the firm have the same one-year-ahead payoffs, they must have identical current market values no avoid arbitrage. Thus, the aggregate fair value of the firm's outstanding debt is \$4.57 million:

$$\begin{aligned} X^{FAIR} &= (.333)(8) - (-1.905) \\ &= \$4.57 \text{ million.} \end{aligned}$$

Note that the current market value of the firm's debt issue is substantially below \$5.71 million, the value at which *riskless* one-year \$6 million face discount debt yields five percent interest. The \$1.14 million differential reflects the premium necessary no compensate the firm's bondholders for bearing the risk of a possible default by the firm should its end-of-period asset value turn our no be "low"

Indeed, the firm's bondholders can view their investment as a combination of riskless one-year \$6 million face debt and a short position in a one-year put option contract on the value of the firm's assets with an exercise price of \$6 million. The short put position is implied since the bondholders of the firm implicitly have granted stockholders, through the limited liability provision, the right no "put" no them the assets of the firm (worth $3 million in the "low" firm value state) in exchange for the $6 million cash par value.

The $1.14 million discount on the firm's *risky'* debt relative no the cost of *riskless* five percent debt is, in fact, *the fair premium* for writing a put on the value of the firm's assets with an exercise price of $6 million with one-year no expiration.

Convertible Debt

A convertible bond obligates the issuing firm either no redeem the bond an par value upon maturity or an the option of the bondholders no permit the bondholder no purchase newly-issued equity an a prespecified price in lieu of the cash par value payment. This prespecified price is called the bond's *conversion prince* because in determines the number of new shares of stock into which the bond can be "converted." If the (fully-diluted) market price of the firm's stock an the maturity date of the bond is higher than the conversion price of the bond, the bond will be converted because the converted stock position is of greater market value than the bond's original par value. If the stock price an maturity is lower than the bond's conversion price, the bondholder will choose the cash par value redemption alternative since conversion in this case would imply a purchase of the firm's stock an a price greater than the price an investor would otherwise face in the open market. In this latter case, of course, the bondholder also bears the risk that the firm tax' default on its redemption of the bond an par value.

Thus, the convertible bond offers participation in the high payoffs no equity in states of the world in which the value of the firm is "high." At the same time, in offers the "insurance" aspect of a straight bond in snares where the value of the firm turns out no be "low."

To show the difference between the valuation of convertible and Non-convertible debt, consider a firm identical no that used in the above example. The only difference is that, besides the one million outstanding shares of stock, in is financed with a convertible instead of a straight debt bond issue, having a par value of $6 million. The conversion price, we will assume, is $5.50 per share. The maturity date payoff no the convertible issue is contingent on rule end-of-year value of the firm's assets.

Again, let us consider two possible end-of period firm asset values, $12 million and $3 million. If the value of the firm turns our robe $3 million, the current stockholders default on repayment of the $6 million par value, and holders of the convertible issue receive total claim no the $3 million in assets. If the value of the firm instead turns out no be ins high value of $12 million, the bondholders can either accept the $6 million cash par value redemption payment or exercise their option no purchase $6 million worth of newly-issued equity an the conversion price of $5.50 a share (thereby creating 1.091 million ($6 million/5.5) new shares)

The decision no convert or non convert depends, of course, upon whether the market value of the 1.091 million new shares of stock received (valued at their fully-diluted price) exceeds the unconverted cash redemption value. If the bond is Converted, the number of shares outstanding will grow no 2.091 million, but the entire $12 million asset value of the firm will be available no the shareholders. The fully-diluted price of the firm's stock would be about $5.74 per share. Thus, the aggregate value of the 1.091 million shares in the converted position would be $6.26 million. Since this sum is $0.26 million greater than the unconverted value of $6 million, the optimal policy for bondholders in the "high" firm value case is no convert.

Given that the maturity value of the convertible will be either $6.26 million (if V^H occurs) or $3 million (if V^H occurs), we can use our general contingent claim valuation formulas no calculate the current fair value of the convertible issue. Substituting $6.26 million for X^H, $3 million for X^L, $12 million for V^H, and $3 million for V^L., we determine that a portfolio equal no 36.23 percent of the firm's assets, combined with $1.82 million in riskless one-year lending an five percent interest, will duplicate the cash flows of the convertible issue. Since this portfolio currently is valued an $4.72 million, the current fair value of the convertible issue also is $4.72 million.

Note that the value of the convertible issue is $0.15 million greater than that of a Non-convertible $6 million discount debt issue of an otherwise identical firm. This differential reflects the value of the call option on the company's assets effectively conferred by convertible debt. *In fact, a convertible bond can be viewed as a combination of nonconnertible debt and a call option contract on a certain proportion of the firm's value.*

The call option contract has an expiration date corresponding no the maturity of the convertible, and an exercise price per share equal no the convertible's conversion price. Furthermore, in delivers a proportion of the firm's value equal no the ratio of the number of shares of stock due the convertible bondholders an the conversion price no the number of shares of stock in the fully-diluted firm. In the current example the aggregate implicit call option contract is written on 52.18 $(^{1091}/_{2091})$ percent of the firm's value, has an exercise price equal no the $6 million face value of the bond, and a time to expiration of one year. The fair value of such a call option contract is $0.15 million—exactly the difference between the fair values of the convertible and Non-convertible issues.

Finally because a convertible bond can be viewed as a Non-convertible bond plus a special call option contract and because a Non-convertible bond itself is actually (as we saw) a combination of a riskless bond and a short pun option on the assets of the firm, a convertible bond ultimately should be valued as a call option plus a risk-free bond and a short pun option position.

Equity Notes

A most recent application of the duplicating portfolio technique for the valuation of corporate securities is the case of equity notes. The equity note is perhaps best described as a "mandatory convertible" instrument. In ins most basic form, in is a fully-collateralized stock purchase contract *obligating* the bearer no buy a specified number of new shares in the issuing firm an some future date (usually ten years from the date of initial issue) The collateral is the par value of an attached coupon-bearing note maturing an the date of the future stock sale. An that date, the note is exchanged for the specified number of stock shares. Because this simple version of the equity note guarantees the future delivery of a fixed number of stock shares, in exhibits the same risk as an equity position and thus will be priced essentially as fully-diluted equity—with one exception: in substitutes *certain* coupon payments on the note for *uncertain* dividend pouts on the stock until the stated stock purchase date.

The equity notes actually issued are structured somewhat differently from the "basic" form to partially mitigate the inherent stock price risk. The number of shares received by the investor at maturity in lieu of the par value of the attached note varies with the actual market price of the stock an that date. The contract specifies two boundary maturity date stock prices: a ceiling price and a floor price. If the actual market price of nine stock tunis our no be equal no or above the ceiling price, rule investor uses the full par value of the note to purchase the firm's shares an the ceiling price (i.e., the investor receives the number of newly-issued shares equal no the ratio of the par value of the note no the ceiling price of the stock purchase contract) If the actual maturity date market price of the stock is between the ceiling price and the floor price, the investor receives the number of shires which, an the going market price, have a market value equal no the par value of the bond. Finally if the stock price is less than the floor price, the investor receives the number of shares equal no the ratio of the par value of the note no the floor price of the contract (i.e., the investor uses the note's full par value to purchase stock an the floor price of the contract) Under this set-up, the investor receives stock with an aggregate marker value greater than, equal no, or less than the par value of the bond as the maturity date stock price turns our no be greater than the ceiling price, between the ceiling and floor prices, or less than the floor price.

While the investor can choose no receive the stock at any time prior no maturity, the provisions of the equity notes observed no date make this event unlikely This is because the coupons foregone by converting typically exceed the dividends gained, and, more importantly because the sliding schedule of stock purchase prices is effective only on the equity none's maturity date. Prior no the maturity date, the purchase price is the ceiling price.

To provide a concrete example of the valuation of an equity note issue, we will once again examine a firm with the same asset value as above. In this case, the firm's capital structure will consist of one million outstanding shares of common stock and a $6 million par value zero-coupon equity note issue maturing in one year. For comparative purposes, we will assume that the ceiling price for the equity note is set an $5.50 per share (identical no the conversion price of the convertible issue discussed earlier), The floor price is assumed no be $4.00 per share. This price structure implies that the total number of new shares to be exchanged for the note issue at maturity can range from 1.091 million (if the maturity date stock price is greater than or equal no $5.50 per share) to 1.5 million (if the stock price is less than or equal no $4.00 per share)

As in our previous applications of the duplicating portfolio pricing technique, we begin by identifying the possible end-of-year payoffs no the equity none which, once again, are contingent upon whether the value of the firm's assets turns out no be $12 million or $3 million. If the firm happens no be worth $12 million an maturity, the value of the equity of the fully-diluted firm will be greater than $5.50 per share so that, under the terms of the collateralized stock purchase agreement, a total of 1.091 million new shares of the firm's stock would be issued no the holders of the equity note issue. The market value of each of the new total of 2.091 million shares of the firm's stock would be about $5.74 12 million of asset value divided among 2.091 million shares) The total value accruing no the original holders of the equity none issue thus would be \$6.26 million (1.091 million shares valued an \$5.74 per share).

If, instead, the end-of-year value of the firm assets turns our no be \$3 million, the value of the firm's fully-diluted equity will be less than \$4 per share 50 that a total of 1.5 million newly-issued equity shares would be transferred no the equity note holders. The market value of each of the new total of 2.5 million outstanding shares of the firm's stock would be \$1.20 (\$3 million of asset value divided among 2.5 million shares) The total value accruing to the original holders of the equity note issue would be \$1.8 million (1.5 million shares valued an \$1.20 per share)

Given that the value of the equity note issue an maturity will be either \$6.26 million or \$1.8 million, we can find the duplicating portfolio for the equity note just as we did for Non-convertible and convertible bonds. In our equity note example, X^H = \$6.26 million and X^L = \$1.8 million so that

$$h^x = \frac{6.26 - 1.8}{12.3} = .496 \text{ and } M = \frac{1}{1.05} [.496 (3) - 1.8] = -\$0.30.$$

Thus, the equity note's duplicating portfolio is a 49.6 percent share of the firm's total existing assets combined with one-year riskless lending of \$0.30 million an five percent interest. The current market value of this duplicating portfolio, and thus the current fair value of the equity note, is \$4. 27 million:

$$X^{FAIR} = (.496)(8.0) - (-.30)$$
$$= \$4.27 \text{ million.}$$

Note that the \$4.27 million fair market value of this \$6 million par value equity note is less than the \$4.72 million fair value of a \$6 million par value convertible issue of an otherwise identical firm. The \$0.45 million premium on the convertible over the equity none reflects the fact that the value of the convertible in the "low" firm asset value snare is higher than that of the equity note (\$3 million versus \$1.8 million)

In general, the difference in value between a convertible bond and a comparable equity note will reflect the difference between the values of the shorn pun positions implicit in the two instruments. The implied pun position of a convertible is a pun on the assets of the firm. The implied pun of an equity none is a put on only a certain proportion of the firm's assets. This proportion is determined by the fraction of total shares in the diluted firm which are delivered no the equity note holders an the floor price. In this example, this floor proportion is 60 percent of a firm's assets.

From our previous analysis we know that the implied pun position of the convertible is worth \$1.14 million. In is straightforward no show that the fair value of the implied pun position of the equity note is \$1.59 million. *Indeed, the difference between these implied put option values is the \$0.45 million differential between the convertible and the equity note derived above.*

The foregoing analyses of the Non-convertible debt, convertible debt and equity note issues highlight the fact that the option pricing model can be applied no corporate claim valuation problems in general. While our specific examples were couched on the "unrealistic" binomial model for end-of-year firm asset values, a more realistic diffusion process assumption can also be used. Diffusion-based valuation models for these corporate claims can be derived no improve upon our binomial models, just as the Black-Scholes option pricing model was an improvement over the binomial option pricing model. (And in the next section, we will demonstrate the application of such a diffusion model no the pricing of an actual equity note issue.)

The basic idea that certain contingent claims contain option-like components also becomes useful in practice when alternative structurings of a security are being considered. For example, we might want no redesign the above equity note issue such than investors would value in essentially as a convertible bond. Our analysis implies, however, that this would occur only if the short pun option position implicit in the equity note was identical no that implicit in the convertible. This would happen only if the number of newly-issued shares granted the equity note holders was large enough no dilute completely the value of the original stockholders' one million share position, such that the equity note holders would acquire the total value of the firm's assets. This condition would be approached only if the floor price of the equity note were set very close to zero.

Empirical Analysis of an Equity Note Issue

In order no test the applicability of the option pricing model no the valuation of equity notes, we used a diffusion-based model no value the equity notes issued by Manufacturer's's Hanover Corporation (MHC) in April, 1982. The issue has a face value of $100 million, matures on April 15, 1992, and carries a percent coupon payable semiannually The contract ceiling and floor prices are $55.55 and $40.00, respectively These contract prices imply that the number of MHC shares no be purchased on April 15, 1992 for the $1,000 face value of each note can range from 18 (an the ceiling price) no 25 (an the floor price) On the day prior no issue, MHC stock closed an $31.75. Thus, the ceiling and floor prices in this collateralized stock purchase agreement were set an premiums of 74.96 percent and 25.98 percent, respectively.

In this analysis, we assume that the total value of MHC's outstanding stock plus its equity notes follows a diffusion process. We will refer to this total value as the firm's value. This is a simplification which allows us to side-step an explicit analysis of the other components of MHC's capital structure. Note, however, that this simplification is still sophisticated enough to capture the essential co-determination of equilibrium stock and equity note values subject to the ultimate uncertainty about their total value.

While the financial theory underlying our model is cast within the same contingent claims framework set forth earlier, the specifics of diffusion-based equity note valuation are too complex no be solved analytically In practice, we can solve for our fair equity note values only with the aid of a computer. The computer solves a system of difference equations approximating a complex differential equation, which in turn characterizes the equity none's value in a diffusion-based contingent claims analysis. In general, the model allows us no quantify he effects of changes in the underlying specifics of he equity note on ins fair value. The model also allows us no compute the fair value of the MHC issue an alternative points in ins trading life.

Thus, we are able no test how well the model explains the actual market prices of this specific issue. Table 3 presents the results of a comparison between actual market prices of the MHC equity note issue and our model's predicted prices for the two-month period between July 1,1982 and August 30,1982.

Columns 2 and 3 present the market values of MHC common stock (per share) and the MHC equity none (per one dollar of face value), respectively Column 4 presents the aggregated value of MHC's stock and ins equity notes (in billions of dollars). Columns 5 through 6 report the calculated fair equity note values given the firm value's (column 4), the time left no maturity of the equity none, the rate of interest, the specifics of the issue (par value, coupon stream, ceiling and floor prices, etc.), the stock's dividend stream, and *two* alternative values of volatility

The volatility input required by the model is the annualized standard deviation of the percentage change in the aggregate market value of MHC stock and equity notes. Ideally we would want no estimate this volatility directly by examining the historical data on the aggregate market value of these two claims. However, since there is no significant trading history for the equity note issue prior no the start of our sample period, we impute this volatility estimate from an historical estimate of the volatility of the return to MHC common stock. For weekly data over the first six months of 1982, this imputed volatility was found no be .22. A slightly higher volatility estimate of .25 is obtained when the historical sample is lengthened no include the data from 1981.[10] We examine the model's equity note values for *both* of these volatility estimates.

We use a riskless interest rate of 13.95 percent in calculating the July model prices, and 13.06 percent in calculating the August model prices. These "axes are the average yields on 10-year Treasury ones for the months of July and August, respectively.

Finally we must make some projection as no the likely dividend stream no be paid on MHC stock over he period ending April 15, 1982, given the information available no the market in July 1982. The 1982 first quarter MHC dividend amounted to $2.92 per hare on an annualized basis. We assume than the market expected dividends to grow an a 7.35 percent compounded annual rate over the equity notes life. This dividend growth rate is the actual percentage dividend increase for 1982 over 1981.

Of the two alternative model price series constructed, the series based upon a volatility input of .22 most closely tracks the actual equity note prices observed in the market. For this volatility estimate, while the model underprice the market values by $1.20 per $100 of face value on average, the root mean squared deviation of the model price from the market price is just 1.6 percent of the average market equity note price. To be sure, significant differences between the model's price and the actual marker price do occur on certain days. Bun most of the larger percentage discrepancies appear when the firm's value is low relative no ins average value. In these cases, model prices show greater downward movement in response no the decrease in firm value than market prices tend no show We do non observe an equivalent phenomenon for higher than average firm values because of the models general tendency towards underpricing.

One reason for this "undershooting" problem may be the simplifying assumption invoked in our specification of the model. The model's performance would certainly be improved if our measure of firm value were expanded no include a more complete picture of MHC's total asset value.

The equity note valuation procedure could be fine-tuned through the incorporation of a more exact total asset value, along with the added rational pricing restrictions. In remains nonetheless a fact than our simple format—using only the market values of the stock and the equity notes itself—explains actual equity note prices within 1.61 percent on average.

The "Components" of an Equity Note

As discussed above, investors can view an equity note position as the sum of three components: a long position in a call option on a certain proportion of the firm's value, a long position in a certain nonconvertible bond, and a short position in a pun option on another proportion of the firm's value. The call option contract has an exercise price equal no the par value of the equity note, and ins expiration date is the same as the equity notes maturity date. The proportion of the firm value controlled in this call option is equal no the ratio of the number of shares of stock due the equity none holders an the ceiling price no the number of shares of stock in the fully-diluted firm. The bond component is a special security which has a riskless maturity date par value, bun a risky coupon stream. The maturity date, par value, and coupon structure of this bond correspond no that of the equity none. Finally, the pun option is written on the proportion of the firm's value determined by the number of shares due the equity note holders an the floor price in the fully-diluted firm. The put's exercise price and expiration date are identical no than of the call.

Table 3 : Model Versus Market Equity Note Values July 1, 1982–August 30, 1982

Date	Market Stock Price ($/Share)	Market Equity Note Price ($/$ of Face)	Firm Value ($ Billions)	Model Equity Note Values ($/$ of Face)	
				Vol = .22	Vol = .25
7/01	26.875	0.940	1.026	.919	.917
7/02	26.625	0.935	1.017	.914	.912

7/06	26.625	0.935	1.017	.913	.911
7/07	26.750	0.935	1.021	.915	.913
7/08	26.625	0.935	1.017	.913	.911
7/09	27.125	0.935	1.034	.921	.919
7/12	28.000	0.950	1.066	.936	.934
7/13	27.250	0.935	1.039	.922	.921
7/14	26.875	0.935	1.026	.916	.914
7/15	26.875	0.935	1.026	.915	.914
7/16	27.125	0.935	1.034	.919	.918
7/19	27.250	0.935	1.039	.921	.919
7/20	28.125	0.945	1.070	.936	.934
7/21	28.750	0.940	1.091	.946	.945
7/22	28.625	0.940	1.087	.944	.942
7/23	28.500	0.940	1.083	.941	.940
7/26	28.125	0.940	1.070	.934	.933
7/27	28.250	0.940	1.074	.936	.935
7/28	28.000	0.940	1.066	.932	.930
7/29	28.250	0.940	1.074	.936	.934
7/30	28.125	0.940	1.070	.934	.932
8/02	28.625	0.950	1.089	.957	.955
8/03	28.625	0.955	1.089	.957	.955
8/04	28.375	0.955	1.080	.953	.951
8/05	28.125	0.955	1.072	.948	.946
8/06	27.500	0.955	1.050	.937	.935
8/09	27.500	0.945	1.049	.936	.934
8/10	27.750	0.950	1.059	.941	.939
8/11	27.125	0.945	1.037	.929	.927
8/12	27.125	0.955	1.038	.930	.928
8/13	27.375	0.960	1.047	.934	.932
8/16	27.625	0.960	1.056	.938	.936
8/17	29.125	0.975	1.109	.964	.962
8/18	29.000	0.975	1105	.961	.960
8/19	27.000	0.950	1.033	.926	.924
8/20	28.250	0.955	1.077	.947	.945
8/23	28.750	0.950	1,094	.955	.953
8/24	28.625	0.950	1.089	.952	.951
8/25	28.250	0.950	1.077	.946	.944
8/26	28.250	0.950	1,077	.946	.944
8/27	26.625	0.940	1.019	.917	.915
8/30	26.250	0.945	1.007	.910	.908
Root Mean Squared Deviation (in percent of average market price) :				1.61	1.77

Firm Value is aggregate market value of stock pulse equity notes (cum accrued interest). Vol. is the measure of volatility applied (see text).

To complete our analysis, we will show how our model distributes an equity note's tonal fair value among these three primary component securities an alternative firm asset values. Table 4 presents the component calculations for the MHC equity none issue as of July 23, 1982. Here we present the breakdown of the model equity none value into ins implicit call, bond, and pun positions—not only for the actual value of the firm on that date (the asterisked row), bun also for other possible values of the firm. Our results are based on the .22 volatility parameter along with the other background assumptions used above.

Table 4 : The Underlying Components of Equity Note Value. July 23, 1983

Firm Value ($ Billions)	Model Value of Equity ($/Share)	Model Value of Equity Note ($/$1 of Face)	Component Values ($/$ of Face)				
			Call	+	Bond	-	Put
0.5	12.56	.620	.001	+	.872	-	.253
0.8	20.72	.799	.014	+	.990	-	.205
* 1.083	28.50	.941	.059	+	1.022	-	.140
1.2	31.72	.999	.088	+	1.027	-	.116
1.5	39.99	1.143	.182	+	1.032	-	.070
2.5	67.53	1.628	.607	+	1.034	-	.013
4.0	108.81	2.366	1.333	+	1.034	-	.002

Row 3 of Table 4 computes the total fair equity none value of $94.1 million on July 23, 1983 (based on the actual firm value of $1083 billion) as the sum of the values of ins three component parts. An this level of firm value, the equity note's value is dominated by ins straight bond value. The net effect of the implicit long call and short pun positions represents only $8.1 million (just about eight percent of face value) If the value of the firm were substantially higher or lower, this result would change. As the value of the firm rises the equity note's value increases for three reasons: first, the call option becomes more valuable as in now has a greater chance of finishing in-the-money; second, the implicit bond position is more valuable since there is less of a chance of default on the risky coupon stream; and third, the short pun position is less of a drag since in is more likely no finish out-of-the-money

Analogous effects on these component values for a decrease in firm value also can be seen. As the value of the firm falls, the call and the bond becomes less valuable and the short pun becomes more of a drag. An some point between firm values of $1.2 billion and $1.5 billion, the two option positions would completely offset each other and the equity note would be priced (for the moment) as if in were a bond with a risky coupon stream, but risk-less par value.

Closing Remarks

This article discusses the potential application of the Black-Scholes option pricing model to the valuation of corporate securities. After outlining the basic elements of the option pricing model, we reviewed how a general contingent claims framework has been used to value corporate debt, both nonconvertible and convertible.

We next explained the model's relevance to the pricing of a relatively new corporate security: the equity note. We then went on to apply the contingent claims model to the valuation of Manufacturer's Hanover's outstanding equity note issue. The model was able to explain market equity note prices within 1.61 percent on average, though certain "large" but short-lived discrepancies did appear during the two-month sample period studied. Finally, we broke down the fair value of this equity note into its three component values: a long call option, long bond, and a short put option. We then showed how each component contributes to the total equity note value as the total value of the firm changes.

The analysis presented here for the MHC equity note issue touches on just a few of the possible uses of the option pricing model for the valuation of corporate claims. The method is useful not only for determining whether a particular security is under or overvalued, but also for simulating the effects of changes in the features of the issue, or changes in the value of the firm, on the value of the security. In designing securities, trade-offs between features of the issue—e.g., coupon rates, conversion premiums, maturity—can be analyzed in a systematic fashion and the net effects on value determined precisely.

In summary, the contingent claims valuation framework is applicable to the pricing of all corporate securities for which the two following conditions obtain: (1) the security's value cab be expressed as a function of the total asset value of the firm, and (2) the total value of the firm can be modelled as a smoothly changing random variable. Applications of this valuation framework to alternative corporate claims are distinguished only by the background work necessary to analyze the differences in the payoff streams of the securities being valued.

5

Corporate Risk Management

In determining their risk management policy, many firms solicit the opinions of investment bankers and commercial lenders. They also pay attention to the yields and ratings on their debt since this gives them direct evidence on how the market perceives their current risk profile. Firms also rely on industry standards in deciding how much debt to issue and how much insurance to purchase.

These approaches are useful because they give the firm access to potentially valuable information about what a "normal" risk profile would look like. But relying too heavily on the opinions of lenders or industry standards doesn't take into account the unique attributes of a particular firm. In many cases, there are no firms whose business breakdown and product market strategy are similar enough to be directly comparable. Even where there is a well-defined industry, this doesn't mean that the risk profiles of other companies are optimal for their current circumstances. For example, there is some evidence that individual debt ratios are, to a large extent, a product of random historical events. Moreover, the potential costs of financial distress to a firm may be quite large, even if the risk to a lender is not that great. If these costs of financial distress are high enough, the fact that, for example, lenders are willing to provide additional funds doesn't mean that the firm should borrow more.

Corporate managements seem to recognize the costs associated with a high risk profile because they engage in a wide variety of risk-reducing behaviour. They buy insurance to protect against property and casualty losses and product liability suits. They use commodity and financial futures and forward contracts to guard against fluctuations in interest rates, foreign exchange rates, and the prices of specific products. They shun risky products, sometimes even when the promised returns are high. And, in many cases, they restrict the amount of financial leverage they employ, even when there may be substantial tax advantages to borrowing.

Typically, these decisions—such as how much fire insurance to buy, whether to hedge a particular foreign exchange risk, and how much leverage to incorporate within the company's capital structure—are made independently of one another, presumably because each deals with a different source of risk. But because each of these decisions affects the total risk of the firm (albeit with different costs and consequences), there are clearly benefits to integrating risk management activities into a single framework. To do this properly, however, requires answers to two major questions: (1) What factors should management consider in deciding the firm's optimal risk profile? (2) What are the relevant trade-offs involved in choosing among the various risk-reducing or hedging mechanisms available? (For example, should one reduce corporate risk by lowering the debt-equity ratio or by taking out a larger product liability policy?)

Unfortunately, modern financial theory offers little guidance in such matters. Indeed, the theory of risk in modern finance, as embodied by the capital asset pricing model (CAPM) and the more recent arbitrage pricing theory (APT), seems to regard as irrelevant, if not actually wasteful, a range of corporate hedging activities designed to reduce the total risk, or variability, of the firm's cash flows. Both the CAPM and the APT demonstrate that, under reasonable circumstances, diversifiable risks are not "priced" by sophisticated investors and, hence, do not affect the stock market's required rates of return. Systematic or "market" risks (those which cannot be diversified away by investors) are priced; but because the price of risk is the same for all market participants, there is no gain to shareholders from "laying them off' to financial markets. Consequently, as this reasoning goes, the expected net present value of buying insurance or a futures or forward contract should be zero in an efficient market, In this light, management decisions to insure or hedge assets appear, at best, "neutral mutations" (having no effect on the value of the firm). At worst, such actions, to the extent they are costly, are viewed as "irrational behaviour" penalizing corporate stockholders,

The purpose of this article is to present and expand upon a relatively new justification for corporate hedging practices—"new," that is, in the academic finance literature. We begin by offering a rationale for actively managing *total* corporate risk that is consistent with both the premise of shareholder wealth maximization and the exclusive focus of asset pricing models on systematic risk. We then go on to use this theoretical framework to generate a set of principles to guide corporate management in establishing a coherent, centralized approach to risk management. Such an approach considers the costs and benefits of a variety of available risk-reducing tools and strategies for managing the total exposure of the company.

Why Total Risk Matters

Modern finance theory holds that the value of a firm is equal to its expected future cash flows discounted at the appropriate interest rate. Financial economists have concerned themselves almost exclusively with the effect of risk on market discount rates, for the most part ignoring its effect on expected cash flow. According to both the CAPM and APT, sophisticated investors require higher rates of return on securities imposing greater risk; but because such investors diversify their asset holdings, they require risk premiums only for bearing systematic (or non-diversifiable) risk. This systematic or "market" risk, generally measured by "beta" under the CAPM, is the sensitivity of a firm's stock price to market-wide price movements. As measured using APT, systematic risk is measured by the sensitivity of market prices to a number of economic factors, such as changes in real interest rates, unexpected fluctuations in GNP growth, and unanticipated changes in inflation.

Finance theory thus implies that stock market investors are concerned not with the total variability of the firm's cash flows (which we shall refer to hereafter as "total risk"), but only with the *co-variability* of those flows with the perform nce of the economy as a whole. Finance theorists have therefore maintained that reducing risks at the corporate level which are diversifiable at the portfolio level does not benefit stockholders. Consequently, the argument goes, most company-specific risks, provided they do not significantly raise the prospect of bankruptcy, can be managed more efficiently by stockholders.

Recent scholarship, however, has argued that although total risk may not affect investors' required returns, large unsystematic risks, if unmanaged, can substantially reduce the value of the firm. In terms of the DCF model of firm value, diversifiable risks may not raise investors' discount rates (the denominator), but they can significantly lower the level of the firm's expected cash flows (the numerator). If this is the case, then reducing total risk can increase expected cash flows, thereby increasing the value of the firm. Given these assumptions, which we think quite reasonable, corporate hedging makes economic sense.

How does higher total risk lower expectations about future cash flows? Firms with higher *total* risk, all else equal, are more likely to find themselves in financial distress. Financial difficulties in turn are likely to disrupt the operating side of the business, reducing the level of future operating cash flows. Perhaps most important, financial distress can give rise to management incentives that conflict with the interests of other parties who do business with the firm; and the adverse effect of such incentives on sales and operating costs is compounded by the risk a version of customers, managers, employees, suppliers, and other corporate stockholders. In addition, variability in corporate earnings can affect a firm's ability to take full advantage of tax credits and write-offs.

The Adverse Incentive Problem

Financial distress, or the threat of bankruptcy, affects management incentives in three fundamental ways. First, managers are more likely to choose high-risk investments that benefit shareholders at the expense of bondholders. Second, they have a tendency to exit promising lines of business or liquidate the entire firm when they would otherwise continue to operate. Third, they may have an incentive to produce goods of inferior quality and provide a less safe work environment for their employees.

A number of finance theorists discuss how the possibility of bankruptcy leads firms to choose possibly sub-optimal investment projects that expropriate wealth from their creditors,They demonstrate that if bankruptcy is likely, the firm's stockholders have an incentive to invest in very risky projects, even if they have negative net present values. This is because the bondholders, rather than the stockholders, bear most of the downside risk from these investments, while the stockholders enjoy most of the gain from the upside potential.

Similarly, one of the present authors shows that financial distress, or the threat of bankruptcy, has an important impact on the firm's liquidation decision and, therefore, on its sales and costs. Managers of financially sound firms, as representatives of stockholder interests, generally will not choose to liquidate the firm because stockholders, as the firm's most junior claimants, receive liquidation proceeds only after other claimants are paid in full. Also, because they will lose their jobs if the firm fails, managers have a more direct incentive to keep the firm in business. As the firm progresses through stages of financial distress toward bankruptcy, however, the firm's creditors exert increasing influence on management decisions; and creditors' priority claim to any liquidation proceeds gives them a much stronger incentive to liquidate the firm. The possibility that a financially distressed firm may be liquidated is shown to reduce the current sales and raise the operating costs of high-risk firms by raising concerns of customers, suppliers, and employees.

Because both stockholders and managers have strong incentives to avoid bankruptcy and liquidation, management may take actions under the threat of financial distress they would not otherwise take. For example, a firm having difficulty raising cash may be tempted to lower the quality of its products and services; they may also cut corners on safety for their employees. These temptations will be especially strong in cases where quality or safety is difficult to monitor from the outside, and where the damage may not come to light immediately. Or, a firm facing financial distress may be tempted to conserve cash by cutting back on research and development, advertising and promotional expenditures, and various forms of working capital such as inventory and receivables.

Thus, while a healthy firm has a strong incentive to produce high-quality products and to take other actions that ensure its long-term viability, these normal incentives are likely to change if the firm is suffering financial distress. Under the threat of bankruptcy, the long-run value of a strong reputation may be less important than generating enough cash to make it through the next day. The cost savings associated with cutting quality levels may be particularly attractive to firms facing creditors threatening to take over and possibly liquidate the firm.

Potential customers and other stockholders anticipate these changes in management incentives and actions. As a result, they become increasingly reluctant to do business with firms in financial distress, as well as with high-risk firms likely to face financial distress in the future. Such expectations of consumers, suppliers, and even employees will adversely affect the firm's future sales, operating costs, and financing costs. In short, the expectation alone of financial distress reduces the expected value of doing business with the firm.

The Effect on Sales

The incentive of companies in financial distress to produce lower quality products will scare off potential customers. This may, in part, explain Chrysler's difficulty in attracting customers when they were on the verge of bankruptcy. In response to this customer hesitancy, Chrysler decided to offer 5-year service warranties on its new cars. This service contract, which may have been very costly to Chrysler, would probably have been unnecessary if Chrysler were not in such financial straits. Certainly, note of its competitors matched its generous terms.

But product quality is not consumers' only worry; service is a major concern as well. If the original supplier goes out of business, parts and repairs may become a problem. This is particularly important where there are economies of scale in producing parts and providing service, The volume of parts for the after market is likely to be far lower than the volume required for the production of new units. Hence, if the firm goes out of business, production volume will drop precipitously, raising the cost and the price of spare parts. Spare parts will also be more difficult to locate. Similarly, the value of investing in specialized training and equipment to repair a particular product will diminish if the product's sales outlook becomes shaky. This means fewer qualified mechanics and more difficulty in finding those who are around.

Thus, reducing total risk can aid a firm's marketing efforts by providing greater assurance to potential customers that the company will be around in the future to service and upgrade its products. Purchasers of long-lived capital assets are especially concerned about the seller's survival.

Potential buyers of Chrysler cars, for example, were understandably nervous about purchasing a product which they might have difficulty getting serviced if Chrysler went bankrupt. Clearly, it is comforting to know that the manufacturer will be there to service the equipment and supply new parts as old ones wear out,

At present, with a shakeout under way in the personal computer business, and with several companies dropping by the wayside, shoppers are more worried about producers' staying power. IBM is exploiting buyers' fears about its competitors' longevity with the message, "What most people want from a computer company is a good night's sleep." The widespread concern about whether companies will be around to service and update their machines threatens further to erode the market shares of smaller producers.

In general, whenever customers face lar (fixed) costs to switching suppliers, the supplie have an incentive to present a low-risk image Switching costs arise when buyers must spend substantial amounts of money tailoring the product their particular needs, which is often the case in purchase of a computer or factory automation equipment. These costs come in the form of specific product adaptations, necessary investments in specialized ancillary equipment, and time spent learni how to operate a supplier's equipment or software.

The importance of having a secure position' the marketplace is evident in the case where outs suppliers provide complementary products services that add value to the firm's product. If supplier must bear a fixed cost to adapt its product work with a new brand, it will first make an assement of the brand's viability in the marketplace, example, software programmes are produced of computers with the largest market share first; only later, if at all, are they rewritten for other brands.

Risk hurts sales for another reason as well as so firms diversify among suppliers in order to reduce disruption to operations in the event that any one supplier is unable to meet its commitments. It takes time to line up new suppliers, ascertain that their products meet required quality standards, negotiate prices and credit terms, establish new shipping routines, and make all the other adjustments necessary to fit a new supplier into the production schedule. The problem of finding new sources of supply becomes more acute during periods of shortage, such as those caused by price controls. Because financial distress can jeopardize a firm's ability to serve as a stable source of supply, riskier, suppliers, all else equal, will gain a smaller share of orders. This is true of suppliers of commodity-type products as well as those of specialized products.

For example, when Wheeling-Pittsburgh Steel Corp filed for bankruptcy in April 1985, customers reduced their orders, the company was forced to discount prices on some products, and suppliers changed their credit terms to cash-on-delivery. One buyer of Wheeling-Pittsburgh's output interviewed by the *Wall Street Journal* said that he wasn't looking for another supplier because his company had multiple sources. But, he added, "If I were singlesourced, I'd have been on the phone two months ago looking for other suppliers."

Risky firms become victims of lost consumer confidence. Customers aren't as willing to do business with a firm that might be going out of business, To some extent, this fear is self-fulfilling as lost sales worsen the firm's financial position and result in a further reduction in sales. Thus, the riskier a firm, the lower its sales are likely to be. Those customers that continue to do business with a risky firm will reduce the price they are willing to pay for the firm's products by an amount equal to their expected damages. As a result, both the unit sales volume and the price received by a firm can be affected by the (perceived as much as the actual) level of its total risk,

AS sales aecune, aistrinution will surter as well, especially for products that cannot just be plugged in, eaten, or worn, Distributors must then invest in training programmes so that their sales people understand and are able to demonstrate the uses of the company's latest products. This fixed cost, in combination with scarce shelf space, limits the number of product lines retailers are willing to carry. The resulting decline in sales further hinders the firm's ability to take advantage of economies of scale, making it less competitive still.

Changes in total risk affect the probability of bankruptcy and, therefore, the possibility that a company will quit a business, Consequently, any action taken by a firm that decreases its total risk will improve its prospects for survival and, hence, its sales outlook.

The Effect on Operating Costs

A firm's cost of doing business is, in part, a function of its suppliers' view of the company's long-run viability. A firm struggling to survive is unlikely to find suppliers bending over backwards to provide it with specially developed products or services, particularly if those products or services are unique and suitable for use only by the firm in question. In general, the value of investing in a long-term relationship with a customer will depend on whether the customer is expected to survive in the long run. The lower the likelihood of future survival, the more of these relationship costs the customer will have to bear up front in the form of higher prices or less closely-tailored services and products.

Lower-risk firms also have an easier time attracting and retaining good personnel. In the event of liquidation, employees must bear search costs, especially where the jon provides tirm-specitic training and skills not easily transferred elsewhere. Higher level managers bear the stigma of being associated with a failure. The more difficult it is for potential future employers to determine the extent of an individual manager's culpability in the corporate failure, the higher the cost attached to this stigma.

The Effect on Financing Costs

The potential for myopic behaviour on the part of the firm extends to its dealings with creditors as well. A company that expects to remain in business will generally be very protective of its credit reputation. The value of a good credit reputation, however, is lower for firms that may not survive to reap the long-run benefits. Such firms have an incentive to borrow money under false pretences and mistreat creditors in order to delay the onset of bankruptcy. Because creditors understand this change in incentives, risky firms will find it more difficult to borrow and obtain credit under favourable terms. Moreover, even if a firm facing financial distress intends to be conscientious in dealing with its creditors, it will have difficulty in assuring them of its intentions.

Firms extenaing trace credit win nave a difficult time imposing sufficiently stringent conditions to assure themselves of repayment. Rather than putting up with the associated risks and problems, they are likely just to cut off trade credit for riskier firms. The potential loss of supplier credits presumably is costly since firms seem to prefer it to most other sources of funds, possibly because it is such a flexible form of financing. (The alternative of negotiating bank loans or other financing every time additional credit is needed imposes a variety of transaction costs on the firm that may be avoided with supplier credits.)

Excessive variability in cash flows could also affect the firm's ability to borrow, Just as a firm facing financial distress cannot be trusted to maintain product quality, so it cannot be trusted to honour its obligation to its creditors. Because of the option-like character of equity shares, shareholders have an incentive to select high-risk projects which increase their wealth by reducing the value of the firm's liabilities. As pointed out earlier, equity holders receive *all* of the upside potential from high-risk investments, whereas bondholders share in the downside losses.

Consequently, the riskier a firm is perceived to be, the more stringent the restrictions lenders will impose on its operating policies and investment projects. These restrictions can prove especially costly for high-growth firms with financing requirements that exceed internally generated cash flow, Moreover, with a risky firm, the interest rate necessary to compensate lenders for the threat that stockholders will yield to temptation may be so high, and the restrictive debt covenants so tightly drawn, as to virtually guarantee that the firm will be unable to pay back its new debts. The result is a drying up of new credits. This could cause the firm to forgo attractive projects, especially if the alternative is an equity issue requiring disclosure of valuable information to competitors.

Decreasing total risk can reduce or eliminate some of the more onerous debt restrictions and covenants. Investment and operating policies with fewer restrictions on them should increase expected future cash flows and shareholder wealth.

The Problem of Risk Aversion

We have already seen one example of how total risk could change the value of the firm as a going concern. Specifically, creditors might push into bankruptcy and liquidation a firm that would otherwise survive. Recognition of this possibility will be reflected in the form of lower sales and higher operating costs,

Less evident is the likelihood that even in a 100 percent equity-financed firm, the firm's value as a going concern will be reduced by large risk exposures. The income streams of most managers and employees are probably not well (or easily) diversified. Consequently, most people will be concerned about the total risk of their job-derived income. The close connection between corporate and personal risk means that a riskier firm must pay employees more to induce them to commit their human capital to the firm, Similarly, suppliers, distributors, and other corporate stockholders will demand to be compensated for bearing added risk, As a result, higher total risk increases the cost of maintaining the organization.

Competition, however, will limit (to the level set by efficient firms) a high-risk company's ability to meet demands for higher compensation. A highly risky firm, therefore, will have difficulty maintaining its organization. The case of AM International is good illustration of the organizational probe posed by financial distress. As the president of one AM's divisions commented, "When you are constantly shifting direction, there is no civility, no culture none of those things that make good companies.' The Multigraphics Division had seven presidents as many years. And 40 executives paraded through the division's six vice-president slots in one four year period.

The reduction in value caused by such disord is especially great for those firms whose principle assets are not physical but intangible—assets, for ex ample, that take the form of organizational skills an assets inseparable from the firm itself, One such ski involves knowledge about how best to service a mar kept, including new product development and adaptation, quality control, advertising, distribution, after sales service, and the general ability to read changing market desires and translate them into salable products. Other valuable organizational asset whose worth would suffer from financial distress-aside from managers with their firm-specific human capital—could include a network of index, pendent distributors or suppliers of specialize products, such as software.

Similarly, many firms are in industries that require sales people to develop close relationship with their customers, Financial distress, which increases a salesman's personal risk, will cause him—whether he is a high-technology sales engineer or a stockbroker—to jump ship, taking customers with them and further eroding the value of the firm. For example, when Cordis, a medical technology firm, found itself in a battle with the Food and Drug Administration (FDA) over the safety of its pacemakers, it suffered serious damage to its sales force, whose members found their commission income plummeting, Many sales people switched to Cordis's competitors. Because of the complexity of pacer technology, sales people tend to have close relationships with the physicians they supply and thus can take their customers along when they switch companies.

Needless to say, the cost to the company from desertion amongst their sales force was considerable,

Moreover, even a temporary increase in risk can do permanent damage to the firm if some stake-holders leave in response to their perception of added personal risk, In order to reconstitute the organization, the firm must bear a variety of fixed costs associated with replacing those risk-averse stockholders. These costs—which include the costs of hiring and training new managers, sales people and other employees, adding new distributors, and finding new suppliers-reduce the value of the firm as an ongoing entity, When disintegration of the organization has progressed far enough, cash flows will turn negative. At this point, shareholders will have no choice but to liquidate the firm, A creditor financed firm will likely be liquidated prior to this point.

Tax Effects

As the variability of operating profits increases, so does the probability that a firm will be unable to make full use of its tax credits and depreciation and interest expense tax deductions. To the extent the resale market in these tax benefits is imperfect (as measured by the discount taken when the tax benefit is sold), an increase in total risk will lead to a reduction in expected corporate cash flows, If the tax credit or tax loss is carried forward, the relevant cost is the reduction in the present value of the tax benefit. By reducing its total risk, a firm can increase the expected value of its tax credits and tax write-offs and thereby increase its expected future cash flows.

Why Total Risk Matters: Summing Up

The negative feedback effect of large corporate exposure to risk on expected cash flow should now be evident. As total risk goes up, the firm's cost of doing business rises, reducing its prospects for survival, The combination of risk aversion and poorer corporate prospects weakens the bonds between the firm and the individuals who comprise the extended organization; and an exodus begins. Distributors switch to other brands, suppliers reorient their production facilities, and firms supplying complementary services and specialized products tailor their products for competing brands. Recognizing this, customers buy less; and the firm's best employees either demand higher salaries or leave, taking their firm-specific knowledge elsewhere, This adds to the firm's risk, which, in turn, further affects the firm's sales and cost of doing business. Thus, there is a natural progression from increased total risk to increased risk of bankruptcy and liquidation. Furthermore, even if liquidation is unlikely, total risk will lower the firm's value by an amount equal to the added cost of organizational maintenance.

To summarize me arguments above, toe true cost of higher corporate risk is the reduction in the value of the firm's tangible and intangible assets caused by the presence (or probability) of financial distress. In general, the greater the value added by the organization to the firm's products or services and the more expensive it is to reconstitute that organization, the greater this cost is likely to be.

Characteristics of Firms With High Costs of Financial Risk

Based on the previous discussion, it is possible to identify specific characteristics of firms for which financial distress is especially costly. Such companies would therefore be likely to benefit most from active management of total corporate risk. Some of these characteristics are industry-specific, based on product type, while others are firm-specific. Industry-specific product characteristics include the following:

1. *Products that require repairs.* This is illustrated by Lee lacocca's response to suggestions that Chrysler declare bankruptcy: "Our situation was unique. It wasn't like the cereal business. If Kellogg's were known to be going out of business, nobody would say: Well, I won't buy their coroflakes today. What if I get stuck with a box of cereal and there's nobody around to service it'?"

2. *Goods or services whose quality is an important attribute but is difficult to determine in advance.* One such service is air transportation. In fact, airline companies in financial difficulty have been hurt by the common belief that they are more likely to cut corners on safety, thereby increasing the risk of an accident,

1. *Products for which there are switching costs.* Such products would include computers or office and factory automation equipment.

2. *Products whose value to customers depends on the services and complementary products supplied by independent companies.* As we saw earlier, many firms require third parties to distribute, sell, service, upgrade, and otherwise add value to their products. Being a low-risk firm helps persuade independent firms to enter into such a symbiotic relationship,

Firm-specific factors include the following:

1. *High-growth opportunities.* Firms having more positive net present value projects available than they can finance with internally-generated funds will jeopardize their access to outside financing by the appearance of being risky. Otherwise, prospective investors could be scared off by the previously-discussed management incentive problems.

2. *Substantial organizational assets.* Firms whose principal assets are intangible—in the form of managers and employees with firm-specific human capital, outside distributors, suppliers, brand names, a reputation for quality and reliability—will have a higher cost of financial distress than firms with mostly physical assets. These intangible assets will rapidly depreciate in value if the firm experiences, or seems likely to experience, financial distress. As firm risk increases, the value of a reputation for quality products diminishes, and managers and other stake-holders are increasingly likely to sever their ties with the firm.

3. *Large excess tax deductions.* Companies such as Chrysler and U.S. Steel cannot take full advantage of their available tax losses, much less the interest on additional debt, Thus, they have less incentive to load up on debt.

Determining the Firm's Risk Profile

A company's optimal risk profile should be determined by trading off the costs of the firm bearing all (or some) of its risks against the costs of somehow hedging or otherwise reducing those risks, In deciding on an appropriate risk profile, management should conduct a comprehensive analysis of all of its significant exposures. The principal focus of this analysis should be on the risk of *cash insolvency—that* is, the probability of running out of cash before meeting debt servicing charges—given a particular risk profile. Cash insolvency is critical because the inability to meet principal, interest, and lease payments may lead to financial insolvency and, ultimately, to bankruptcy.

However, the analysis can and should be extended to examine the firm's capacity, under various risk scenarios, to service fixed charges of any kind, For example, those firms that perceive large costs to cutting preferred and common stock dividends will treat these as a fixed cost. Strategic factors also enter here. Firms with substantial growth opportunities will often prefer to maintain a continuous research and development programme, and to fund substantial advertising and other marketing expenditures, in both good times and bad.

The Worst Case Scenario

Unfortunately, the difficulty of performing a thorough cash flow analysis may lead firms to limit themselves to using rules of thumb, usually based on various coverage ratios, But coverage ratios do not tell a financial manager what is most important: the probability of cash insolvency associated with alternative risk profiles. This requires a series of cash budgets prepared assuming (1) different economic conditions and (2) the levels of usage of different risk-reducing mechanisms. To do this properly, the financial manager must specify a range of likely future economic scenarios and how the firm's cash flows will be affected by these developments, with a probability attached to each scenario, Moreover, it is necessary to determine other possible sources of cash besides the cash flow from operations. This includes liquid assets that can be drawn down, accounts payable that could be stretched, expenditures that could be deferred, and assets that could be sold. The end result is a series of net cash flows that are or can be generated under each of the different economic scenarios, Based on the associated probabilities, the financial manager can then examine these cash flows and see whether a particular risk profile exposes the firm to too much financial risk. A useful place to begin determination of an appropriate risk profile is to analyze what happens to a firm's cash flows under a "worst case scenario." This could mean a general or industry recession when sales are severely depressed, but it could be any combination of adverse circumstances. For example, a company with a sizable export market, such as Rolls Royce, might be especially concerned with the effects of a product recall.

In 1961, gordon Donaldson presented a framework for evaluating corporate debt capacity that can be easily adapted (and , in fact, may actually be better suited) to the task of quantifying total corporate risks. In order to use Donaldson's method for this purpose, management would begin by identifying the various sources of risk to which the firm is exposed. Then, for each of these categories of risk, net cash flows can be calculated assuming the worst happens; and, at the end of this process, management will have an estimate of the cash balance the firm can reasonably expect to have at the end of the recession (or some firm-specific catastrophe), specifically, this means estimating

$$CB_r = CB_0 + NCE_r$$

where

CB_r = the cash balance at the end of a recession

CB_0 = the cash balance at the start of a recession

NCE_r = the net cash flow during the recession.

By doing this calculation for a range of possible net recessionary cash flows, this information can be used to construct a probability distribution of the ending cash balance, CB_r.

The next step in this analysis is to compare these cash flows to fixed charges. Then for each increment of debt, insurance, forward contracts and the like, the firm could determine the probability of cash insolvency based on the probability distribution of CB_r.

Suppose, for example, that a firm normally maintains $1 million in cash and marketable securities. This is the cash balance that would be on hand at the start of a recession or the onset of some other adverse circumstances. Assume that such an economic decline, when it comes, is expected to last for two years. To show the effects of additional debt on the firm's risk profile, assume it borrows an additional $5 million, with annual debt servicing charges of $1.5 million. Its cash balance at the end of the economic decline will be

$$CB_r = \$1{,}000{,}000 - (2 \times \$1{,}500{,}000) + NCF_r.$$
$$= -\$2{,}000{,}000 + NCF_r$$

Hence, the probability of cash insolvency under this financing plan equals the probability that net cash flow under adverse conditions will fall below $2 million. Management must then decide how high a probability of cash insolvency it is prepared to tolerate. (This judgment should not be based on its own preferences alone, but rather on what would add most value to shareholder.)

Cash Inadequacy

Thus far, our analysis of the firm's ask profile has been in terms of the probability of cash insolvency. But long before reaching this point, the firm could be in serious financial trouble. More important, as we saw earlier, this financial distress can prove very costly for certain types of firms, especially those with substantial amounts of organizational assets.

This means that the risk analysis should be extended to deal with the case of *cash inadequacy,* defined by Donaldson as the inability to fund all desired, but not absolutely essential, expenditures. This category would include items such as dividends, an R&D programme, expenditures to upgrade plant and equipment, and advertising and other marketing costs. By this point, the company is cutting into muscle and bone; and this will affect its ability to sustain whatever competitive advantage it has. The result will be lower expected future operating cash flows, which will be reflected in a lower stock price today.

Table 1 : Inventory of Financial Resources

	Available for use within		
Resources	**One quarter**	**One year**	**Three years**
Uncommitted reserves			
Instant reserves			
Surplus cash	$_______		
Unused line of credit	$_______		
Negotiable reserves			
Additional bank loans	$_______		
Issue of long-term debt		$_______	
Issue of new equity			
Preferred stock		$_______	
Common stock		$_______	
Reduction of planned outflows			
Volume related			
Change in production schedule	$_______		
Scale related			
Marketing programme		$_______	
R&D budget		$_______	
Administrative overhead		$_______	
Capital expenditures		$_______	
Value related			
Dividend payments		$_______	
Liquidation of assets			
Sales of assets			
Land and real estate		$_______	
Equipment		$_______	
Accounts receivable		$_______	
Inventory		$_______	
Sales of business units			$_______
Total financial resources available	$_______	$_______	
		$_______	$_______
			$_______

Source : Donaldson (1971), "Strategy for Financial Emergencies" *Harvard Business Review* (November-December), p.72.

Table 1 shows the various ways in which firms can mobilize financial resources in the event of a liquidity problem. These financial resources can be categorized into uncommitted reserves, reductions of planned expenditures, and liquidation of assets. The first category includes excess cash and marketable securities, unused lines of credit, and other sources of liquidity that can be readily accessed. If these sources prove insufficient, the firm can then begin cutting certain non-essential expenditures. Provided the firm is already operating in an efficient manner, these cuts will trade off future cash flows for current cash. Finally. the firm can sell off some of its assets. Again, if the firm was already being run in a lean manner, these asset sales will harm future profitability. The costs associated with these various forms of cash inadequacy and insolvency must be traded off against the costs of reducing risk

Methods of Reducing Total Risk

There are many ways in which firms can reduce their total risk, though some are clearly less costly than others, Depending on the methods used, a firm's cost of achieving a given level of risk reduction can vary widely, Management thus has an incentive to select carefully the most cost-effective method of dealing with total risk.

The methods for managing corporate risk can be broken down into two basic categories:" financial" and real." The principal risk-reducing techniques that can be categorized as financial include lowering the firm's debt-equity ratio, buying or selling forward or futures contracts, and buying insurance. Real adjustments include the adoption of production processes that reduce the degree of operating leverage, avoidance of high-risk projects, and abandonment of existing high-risk products (such as those subject to large liability suits for which no adequate insurance is available).

Restricting the Debt-Equity Ratio

The finance literature is replete with references to the effect of debt financing on the firm's total risk, By restricting its debt ratio, the firm will reduce its degree of financial leverage, thereby decreasing the probability of financial distress and bankruptcy. In the limit, the all-equity firm would virtually eliminate the probability of bankruptcy.

The fact that we see very few all-equity financed firms suggests that this risk-reducing technique is not costless, In particular, because interest payments come out of before-tax income whereas dividends are paid out of after-tax income, debt may be a less expensive source of financing, at least up to a certain point. Hence, the loss of the interest tax shield provided by debt serves as a disincentive to firms to lower their total risk by means of debt reduction. At the same time, however, the tax advantage of debt gives firms an incentive to use other methods of reducing total corporate risk, enabling them to add still more debt to their capital structures. This may allow them to increase their debt tax shield without significantly raising the probability of financial distress.

Futures and Forward Contracts

A futures or a forward contract calls for delivery, at a fixed future date, of a specified quantity of a given commodity—be it foreign exchange or orange juice—with the price fixed at the time the contract is set. With a forward or futures contract, a firm can lock in its future cost of inputs or sales revenue. For example, an orange juice manufacturer can hedge against the possibility of price fluctuations in its basic raw material by buying orange juice futures. Similarly, a copper mining firm can lock in the revenues from a new mine by selling the output in advance through use of a copper futures contract.

The cost of a forward or futures contract is simply the cost of executing the transaction. In the case of a forward contract, the cost is the spread between the bid and ask price. With a futures contract it is the opportunity cost of the margin amount plus the trading commissions. In a large, active, and well-organized market, such as the foreign exchange market, these costs are likely to be minimal. In other words, the net present value of a futures or forward contract traded in such a market is close to zero. (But, at the same time, the benefits to the corporation from reducing total risk could be substantial.)

Insurance

Buying insurance is a standard approach to hedging corporate risk. The basic problem with insurance is the large load embedded in its price; that is, insurance rates include a premium over and above the expected losses associated with the policy in order to cover marketing and claims servicing costs, as well as the implicit costs of moral hazard and adverse selection.

Insurance firms do have a comparative advantage in some areas of risk management, such as efficiency in claims service and evaluating safety projects. In addition, the purchase of insurance can act as a signal to debt holders and other claimants that the firm's investment decisions will be geared toward maximizing the value of the firm rather than the value of the firm's equity.

Those firms for which the cost of risk is not that great, based on the characteristics described in Section 2, will choose to self-insure more of their risks. But it should be emphasized that the decision not to insure risks with an insurance company is not the same as choosing to self-insure. The firm has many other means available to reduce risk. It should use insurance only when the costs to insurance compare favourably with the costs of other risk-reducing techniques.

Avoiding High Risk Projects

The easiest way to manage risk is to avoid it, which firms can do by screening out high-risk projects. The ease of this approach, however, masks potentially high opportunity costs. The real issue is the degree of risk a company is willing to tolerate and the return required to bear it. A policy of avoiding risky investments ignores the potentially high returns available and the extent to which a firm can control risk in other ways. After all, companies are in business to take risks, provided such risks are recognized, intelligently managed, and promise to be compensated through adequate returns.

In judging the value of undertaking an investment, however, is must be recognized that a project that adds excessive risk to the firm's overall project portfolio may cause financial trouble, and thereby jeopardize all its other activities. An example of this is the case of the Johns Manville Corporation. The high risk associated with its asbestos division resulted in huge product liability suits directed against Johns Manville, A. H. Robbins (the Dalkon shield), and other companies. Their response more often than not is to avoid making those products that may subject them to similar liability lawsuits in the future, again, however, as pointed out above, the opportunity cost of such a policy may be very great.

While some firms may choose to drop overlay risky projects or products, there are less drasitic steps that can be taken. Since it is the project's contribution to the riskiness of the firm's portfolio of projects—that matters, one alternative is to choose projects with cash flows that are negatively correlated, thereby hedging or insuring the cash flows of the other projects. Conversely, firms could avoid choosing projects with returns that are highly correlated because of the added likelihood of bankruptcy.

The latter strategy is not costless, however. In vestments with differing cash flow patterns are most likely to be those in businesses outside of management's area of expertise, which of course increases the probability that the investments selected will have negative net present values. But, even an investment with a negative NPV when evaluated standing alone may have a positive NPV when account is taken of the beneficial effects of risk reduction on the firm's other project cash flows.

Firms can also reduce the correlation among project returns without venturing into new businesses by diversifying internationally. The relevant issue is whether diversification is the least costly form of risk reduction. For example, firms can also reduce total risk by designing their projects to have lower operating leverage, a subject we turn to now.

Reducing the Degree of Operating Leverage

Just as reducing the degree of financial leverage lowers total risk, so too does reducing the degree of operating leverage. And for the same reason: it reduces the ratio of fixed to variable costs. For example, if workers can be laid off or fired with relative ease, the more labour-intensive the production process selected, the higher the variable cost-fixed cost ratio, and so the lower the firm's risk. But, if a more capital-intensive production process has lower expected costs, the benefits of risk reduction can come at a high price, similarly, a firm may forgo the opportunity to take advantage of economies of scale because of the attendant increase in its degree of operating leverage; it may choose instead to build a scaled-down plant that has higher unit costs but involves less risk. In both cases, however, competitors who select the more efficient process will have a cost edge they can use to great advantage.

Long-term sales contracts provide a possible solution to this dilemma. By entering into such a contract, particularly of the "take-or-pay" variety with a minimum floor price, the firm can take advantage of the lower expected cost of the large-scale, capital-intensive process while at the same time reducing its total risk. But if a long-term contract involves simply a transfer of risk to customers, they will demand a price discount for bearing this risk. Under plausible circumstances, however, both the producer has a guaranteed outler for its goods while the customer has a stable source of supply.

In some instances, it is not possible to reduce the degree of operating leverage by altering the labour-to-capital ratio. For example, as long as an airplane is in service, it requires a full crew; that is, its ratio of labour to capital is fixed. As another example, labour is a fixed cost for many Japanese firms because they provide lifetime employment for their workers. Thus, changing the labour-to-capital ratio does not change a Japanese firm's degree of operating leverage.

The alternative in these instances is to convert a portion of the worker's income from a strictly contractual claim into a residual or equity claim. This can be done by typing a substantial portion of the worker's expected income to the firm's profitability. Thus, for example several airlines facing financial difficulty have lowered pay levels while offering higher expected bonuses; others have give their employees stock in lieu of higher pay. similarly, in Japan, most employees receive on the order of one third their annual income in the form of a year-end bonus tied to the firm's profitability during the year.

Trade-offs Among Risk-Reducing Mechanisms

Choosing among the various risk-reducing techniques described in the previous section involves several considerations, We begin this section by offering a few basic principles of risk management:

- First, since the management of total risk entails real costs, the firm should be prepared to pay a positive price to reduce risk.
- Second, the optimal level of risk the firm's risk-bearing capacity is found at the point at which the cost of reducing an additional unit of risk is just equal to the benefit from that incremental degree of risk reduction.
- Third, the firm should take advantage of any opportunities to reduce risk at a zero net cost, Needless to say, the firm should seize any risk-reduction bargains; that is, any opportunities to reduce risk at a below-market price. Such bargains are generally to be found, for example, in the form of government-subsidized insurance, such as political risk insurance or export credit insurance.
- Fourth, the firm must bear in mind that real adjustments to reduce risk usually entail real costs, whereas some financial adjustments, such as the use of forward or futures contracts, may be undertaken at a minimal cost.

- Fifth, the firm must take into account the comparative advantages in risk bearing of different institutions. A large multinational industrial firm may have sufficient diversity of operations to self-insure risks ordinarily transferred to an insurance company.
- Sixth, the firm should take into account the effect that reducing one form of risk can have on another form of risk.

The last point, especially, bears some elaboration. Supposes for example, General Electric sells jet engines to Lufthansa with payment due in one year and set in deutsche marks, GE can hedge its currency risk on this transaction by selling an equivalent amount of deutsche marks forward for dollars for one year. But this does not mean that all risk is eliminated. By transforming a deutsche-mark denominated contract into a U.S. dollar-denominated contract, use of the forward contract is substituting exposure to inflation risk for exposure to currency risk. Without hedging, GE will know how many deutsche marks it will receive in one year, but it won't know the dollar value of those deutsche marks, By hedging, GE will lock in a dollar price for its receivable, but it will not know the purchasing power of those future dollars.

The choice of hedging or not hedging, therefore, depends on which is the bigger risk, inflation risk or currency risk. For most countries with moderate inflation, the answer will surely be currency risk. But for hyper in flationary countries such as Brazil or Mexico, the future purchasing power of the local currency will be less certain than the future purchasing power of the dollar or other strong currency. In this situation, currency risk will be less of a concern than inflation risk.

Similarly, hedging one end of a transaction without hedging the other could result in more risk than not hedging. Suppose Trader Joe buys 4,000 bottles of French champagne to be delivered and paid for in 90 days. The French franc (FF) price is FF100 per bottle which, at the current spot rate of FF1 = $.11, is equivalent to $11 a bottle. If the 90-

day forward rate is $105, TraderJoe can lock in a dollar cost of $10.50 per bottle.

But suppose Trader Joe buys French francs forward to pay for its purchase and the franc depreciates to $09, while the price of French champagne remains at FF100 per bottle. Trader Joe will now be facing competition from other wine importers whose cost per bottle is only $900, $1.50 below its own cost. This competitive pressure will drive down the price at which Trader Joe can sell its champagne. Thus, if it hedges its future purchases of champagne, Trader Joe's dollar profit margin will be hurt by a franc depreciation.

Of course, it will benefit from an appreciation of the franc. The important point, though, is that hedging in this case actually increases the variability, and hence the risk, of Trader Joe's profit margin. The reason is that hedging will fix Trader Joe's dollar cost while its dollar price will vary in line with the dollar value of the franc. By not hedging, Trader Joe's dollar cost and dollar revenue will move in unison, thereby preserving a relatively constant dollar margin.

Reducing the Costs of Risk

An alternative approach to risk management is to reduce the costs associated with risk. There are several ways of doing this, each of which can be used in conjunction with any of the risk-reducing mechanisms discussed previously.

Merger with a Larger, More Financially Stable Company

A small firm with an innovative product but in a precarious financial position can strengthen its marketing effort by linking up with a larger, less risky company. Potential customers will realize that the company's prospects have improved and worry less about whether its product will be serviced and upgraded in the future. Thus, total cash flows of the two firms joined together will exceed the sum of their cash flows operating independently not because of any synergistic effects but because customers perceive less risk in buying the new product or service. Additionally, mergers lead to lower total risk because of diversification, which may benefit the acquiring firm's existing marketing efforts.

Product Compatibility

Another possibility is to produce equipment compatible with the leading manufacturer's product line. Then, even if the original producer becomes financially distressed, there will still be a large support network. Service and spare parts should be readily available and there should be a ready secondary market for the product. This strategy, however, forces companies to compete on the basis of production cost, hurting those firms with a competitive advantage in the design and development of novel products. For example, if Apple Computer had followed the strategy of IBM-compatibility, it work never have brought out its innovative Macintosi personal computer. Also, those so-called plug compatible" companies (those producing IBM-compatible equipment) have faced enormous risks because their destinies are largely controlled by IBM.

Off-the-Shelf Components

In line with the previous discussion, the firm can use off-the-shelf components and other readily available product inputs to reduce the cost to its suppliers of financial distress. In the event the firm goes out of business at a later date, the alternative of using specialized inputs could impose heavy costs on suppliers, in the form of plant and equipment and inventory unsuitable for other uses. On the other hand, the decision to stick to off-the-shelf items could prove costly since it limits the firm's design options.

Training Programmes

As pointed out earlier, a major cost of financial distress to employees is that the value of their firm-specific human capital will be greatly diminished should they be forced to seek employment elsewhere. Firms can reduce this cost by providing opportunities to their employees to develop their human potential so it is applicable to a wider variety of circumstances. For example, Procter and Gamble's reputation for providing employees with a postgraduate education in consumer marketing has enabled it to attract top-flight talent. The portability of this knowledge is evidenced by the large numbers of P & G alumni holding top marketing positions in other firms (though such a policy, by making its employees more mobile, is likely to result in increased turnover with all its attendant costs).

Using Manufacturers' Representatives

Salespeople who specialize in only one product line face a good deal of personal risk in the event something happens to that line. They will demand to be compensated for bearing this risk. An alternative to hiring in-house salespeople is to use manufacturers' representatives who handle a variety di products and lines, This diversification reduces their personal risk and lowers the amount of compensation they demand. The cost of using manufactures' reps, of course, is that the firm's products may not be adequately represented and serviced.

Summary and Conclusions

The basic message of this paper is that corporate cash flows are influenced by the firm's risk profile. Its revenues, operating costs, financing costs, taxes, and future investment opportunities will all be affected by the likelihood of financial distress, which in turn is a function of total risk, consequently, even though finance theory maintains that reducing total risk will not lower the firm's required rate of return, it should lead to an increase in corporate cash flows.

For this reason, firms should carefully consider hedging and other risk-reducing activities. Because these activities may be costly, however, it is necessary to balance their costs against the benefits of risk reduction. In particular, the optimal level of risk–the firm's *risk capacity* , if you will—is found at the point at which the cost of reducing an additional unit of risk is just equal to the benefit from that incremental degree of risk reduction. In other words, the firm's risk capacity is defined as the amount of risk it should bear, as distinguished from the amount of risk it could support.

The risk capacities of firms vary widely given the different natures of the markets they operate in and the strategies they pursue. Some of the characteristics of firms for which financial risk is most costly are others are firm-specific. Industry-specific product characteristics that indicate a high cost of financial distress include the following:

- Products that require periodic repairs.
- Goods or services whose quality is difficult to determine in advance.
- Products for which there are switching cost.
- Products whose value to customers depends on the services and products supplied by independent companies.

Firm-specific factors include the following:

- High-growth companies.
- Substantial amounts of organizational assets.
- Large excess tax deductions.

Firm with high costs of financial distress have relatively low risk capacities and should use the various risk-reducing techniques suggested in this paper. These techniques can be characterized as either "financial" or "real" Financial techniques include limiting the use of debt, buying insurance, and buying or selling forward or futures contracts. Real adjustments include adopting production processes that reduce the degree of operating leverage, avoiding high-risk capacities and, hence, can afford to be more highly leveraged, undertake riskier projects, and self-insure.

In choosing these risk-reducing techniques the firm should take advantage of any opportunities to reduce risk at a zero cost. One consideration that should be borne in mind is that real adjustments to reduce risk usually entail real costs, whereas some financial adjustments, such as the use of forward or futures contracts, may be undertaken at minimal cost. Moreover, the firm should take into account the effect that reducing one from of risk can have on another form of risk. For example, entering into a fixed-price contract eliminates relative price risk but may introduce a significant exposure to inflation risk. It is these kinds of interdependent exposures that an integrated approach for managing corporate risks can recognize and deal with.

6

Corporate Insurance Decision

Introduction

In 1980, American corporations paid more than $49 billion in property and liability insurance premiums. When set against the roughly $63 billion in corporate dividend payments during the same year, these insurance purchases seem particularly significant. Yet, in spite of the magnitude of these numbers, there has been little careful analysis of the decisions leading to such large expenditures. The finance and economics literature has devoted scant attention to the topic. There is, to be sure, a large separate body of academic insurance literature which purports to explain the corporate demand for insurance. But the approach of this insurance literature, we will argue, is fundamentally flawed.

We think there are useful answers to the question of why companies buy insurance, answers consistent with economic logic and the theory of modern finance. But these answers are less obvious than those that have been furnished by recognized authorities on insurance. Our approach also provides explanations of some fairly recent developments in corporate insurance: the appearance of retroactive liability coverage, in which companies purchase additional coverage *after* major disasters; the use of 'claims only" insurance contracts, whereby insured companies pay for the services of an insurance company while bearing themselves the risk of losses through claims; and the growing trend toward self-insurance, reflected both in the use of higher deductibles and the establishment of captive insurance companies.

But, before examining the competing arguments for corporate insurance, let's take a careful look at what an insurance policy does.

The Economics of Insurance

Insurance does not eliminate risk; it is a contract which simply transfers risk from the policyholder to an insurance company In return, the insurance company, of course, demands a premium. The real cost of insurance, called the "loading feel" is the difference between the premium and the expected payoff. As that difference increases, insurance becomes less attractive.

Let's begin by assuming that the decision to purchase insurance, whether by corporations or by individuals, is *solelj'* a decision to transfer risks from the policyholders to an insurance company From the perspective of financial economics, this decision is justified only when the insurance company has a comparative advantage in bearing the risks in question. Such an advantage can derive from several sources :

(1) from the reduction of risk achievable by pooling a large portfolio of risks, for which the expected loss is highly predictable;
(2) from superior access to capital markets; and
(3) from expertise acquired through specialization in evaluating and monitoring certain kinds of risks.

Now, we relax our initial assumption to allow that companies might be buying insurance for reasons other than to transfer risk. The expected payoff of the policy generally contains two components :

(1) the monetary indemnity the insurer pays if a loss occurs, and
(2) any services provided by the insurer

Under the policy. The distinction between monetary indemnity and service provision is important because, in types of insurance where relatively more services are provided, a larger difference exists between the premium and the expected indemnity. In other words, because a significant portion of the premium paid is used to provide the services rendered in conjunction with the policy, a relatively smaller portion will be used to satisfy claims. Thus, a fourth source of insurance companies' comparative advantage would be their specialization and economies of scale in providing services such as claims administration and settlement.

Only the last two are the exclusive province of insurance companies; and thus, only they are likely to constitute the principal comparative advantage of insurance companies over the large, widely-held corporations they insure. And the fact that some of the largest corporations have chosen to develop their own insurance expertise—or to form their own insurance captives—suggests that, in many cases, even these two advantages are not that significant.

The Important Difference between Individual and Corporate Insurance

Before proceeding further with the question of the corporate demand for insurance, we want to consider first the simplest case: the purchase of insurance by individuals. Why do individuals buy insurance? Most people are "risk averse." 2 Insurance contracts allow them to hedge risks, reducing uncertainty And it is not hard to see that, relative to the risk-hearing capacity of insurance companies, the utility of most individuals to self-insure against large risks is severely limited. The private assets of individuals are not protected by the "limited liability" clause which shelters the other assets of corporate stockholders. Thus, decisions by individuals to pay premiums to insure their hard assets and human capital are economically "rational" choices based primarily on insurance companies' advantages in averaging, and thus "diversifying away," such risks.

Private or closely-held corporations are likely to purchase insurance for the same reason—namely, their limited ability to bear certain risks relative to the risk-hearing capacity of insurance companies. The owners (who are also, of course, risk-averse") of such companies often have a large proportion of their wealth invested in the firm; find, whether out of a desire to maintain control or some other motive, they do not fully diversify their own holdings. So, for many closely-held and private companies, logic and experience tell us that the companies' owners will self-insure only where they have specialized expertise and, thus, their own kind of comparative advantage.

The case of large, widely-held corporations, however, presents some important differences which the standard insurance literature has failed to acknowledge. The conventional wisdom says, in effect, that because the owners of corporations (their stockholders and bondholders) are risk averse, a prudent financial manager should attempt to minimize the corporate owners' exposure to risk. This prescription does not necessarily imply that will risks should be insured. For example, the standard theory rightly holds that a large national car rental agency like Hertz, should not purchase collision insurance on its automobiles. With its large fleet of cars, Hertz can eliminate its collision risk, just as an insurance company does, by pooling its risks and averaging its losses. The purchase of collision insurance by Hertz would thus not only he needless duplication, but the payment of the "loading fees" built into the premiums would represent an outright loss to the command.

But, in the case of a large corporation with a smaller fleet of more expensive vehicles, the conventional rationale for corporate insurance—which, again, holds that the underlying source of the corporate demand for insurance is risk-aversion—would argue for insuring those corporate assets. Because such a company does not have the ability to eliminate its collision risks by averaging, the owners are exposed to risk. Such risks, so the reasoning goes, are better borne by insurance companies; and thus the corporation should purchase collision insurance.

The conventional explanation, however, is inadequate because it fails to recognize that the companies stockholders and bondholders have the incentive and the ability to diversify their own portfolios of corporate securities; and in so doing, they can and do eliminate precisely the kinds of risks that are insurable through an insurance company.

Stockholders and bondholders, on average, hold a lot of different securities because they are aware of the benefits of diversification. As the owners of corporate assets, they bear risks in many dimensions: some are insurable risks and some are not. By combining many securities in a portfolio, investors can effectively eliminate most insurable corporate risks by "averaging across many securities—just as Hertz averages its automobile collision risk. The theory of finance tells us that because stockholders and bondholders can cheaply eliminate insurable risks by diversifying their own holdings, the corporate purchase of insurance for the sole purpose of reducing investors' exposure to risk is redundant; and, furthermore, it imposes needless costs on the company's stockholders.

One of the cardinal principles of modern finance is that, on average and over long periods of time, investors both expect and receive rewards commensurate with the risks they bear. As the bulk of the academic evidence also shows, however, average returns on investment correlate most strongly with what is known as 'systematic' or "non-diversifiable" risk. The measure of this risk, known as 'beta,' is a measure of the sensitivity of individual stock prices to market-wide and general economic developments; and such risk cannot be reduced or eliminated by investors' diversification of their holdings. Nor, of course, is a company's "systematic" risk likely to he reduced by purchasing insurance—because insurable risks, to the extent they have no discernible correlation with broad economic cycles, are completely 'diversifiable' for investors.

The capital markets, as logic would suggest, do not reward companies for eliminating "diversifiable" risks: Why should investors pay a premium for managements' reducing exposures to risk which rational investors have already eliminated through their own diversification? By reducing or eliminating diversifiable—and thus most insurable—risks, a company does not reduce the market's perception of its required rate of return or 'cost of capital."

Thus, the prices of its stocks and bonds are not likely to be affected by the presence or absence of insurable risks. Consequently, just as in the Hertz case, the purchase of insurance by a corporation for the sole purpose of reducing insurable risks for the stockholders and bondholders would be redundant. It would also be a waste of stockholder funds because the premium charged for the insurance will not be actuarially fair. For the widely-held corporation, then, where the owners have the incentive and the means to provide their own kind of self-insurance through diversification, the logic of modern finance says that corporations should not purchase insurance—not, at least, for the conventional reasons.

A Rationale for Corporate Insurance

At the same time, however, we believe there are important incentives that provide for a *rational* corporate demand for insurance, incentives which have nothing to do with investors' aversion to risk. In the remainder of this article, we will argue that this demand derives from the ability of insurance contracts to provide corporations with :

(1) low-cost claims administration services;
(2) assistance in assessing the value of safety and maintenance projects;
(3) an improvement in their incentives to undertake investments in such projects;
(4) a means of transferring risk away from those of the company's claim holders who are at a disadvantage in risk-bearing; and
(5) a reduction of the company's expected tax liability.

We also briefly analyze the special case of regulated companies, which have some additional incentives for buying insurance.

Efficiency in Claims Settlement

Examining more closely the services provided under insurance contracts can provide a partial answer to the question of why corporations purchase insurance. Most obviously, insurance companies develop a comparative advantage in processing claims, an advantage which derives from specialization and from economies of scale. Accordingly, we would expect the corporate demand for insurance to be explained, at least in part, by insurance companies' relative expertise and efficiency in providing low-cost claims administration services.

The most striking confirmation of our argument is the existence of special "claims only" insurance contracts. Under the terms (if a "claims only" contract, the insurance company provides only claims management services, while the firm pays all the claims. There is no transfer of risk between the insured and the insuring company. We would expect such policies to be used by companies experiencing a large number of claims. In such cases, a "claims only" policy not only allows the insured company to pool and average its own risks; it also reduces the average cost of settling claims by enabling the insured company to pool and average its own risks; it also reduces the average cost of settling claims by enabling the insurance company to use its network of claims administrators more intensively

One of the problems that could arise from a "claims only" arrangement is that the insurance company would lose its incentive to negotiate the best possible settlement, because it no longer has to pay the indemnity But when claims are numerous, the insured company should be in a good position to review and evaluate the settlement record. This in turn should enable the insured to monitor the insurer's effectiveness in holding down the costs of claims. By contrast, in those cases where claims are relatively infrequent, it would be more difficult for the insured company to monitor the efficiency of the claims settlement procedure. In such cases, we expect to see standard policies where the insurer provides both claims administration and the indemnity.

Liability insurance provides another example of claims settlement services provided by the insurance companies. A liability insurance policy not only indemnifies the policyholder if a valid claim is presented, it also provides legal representation when the insured is faced with a suit. If the suit is for less than the policy limit—as is the case in most suits–the policyholder has little incentive to engage quality legal services. We suspect that it is largely because of these incentives, as well as insurance companies' greater familiarity with claims negotiations and settlements, that providing legal representation has become a standard part of liability insurance contracts.

In the unusual case where the suit greatly exceeds the limit on coverage, the roles—and thus the incentives—are reversed. Because the insurance company's liability is limited under the policy, it has less incentive to negotiate an efficient settlement. Consider, for example, the following case reported in the *Wall Street Journal*:

When the fire bit the MGM Grand hotel in Las Vegas last November 21, killing 85 persons, the hotel's owner had 530 million in liability insurance. Since then the hotel company has increased its liability coverage to nearly 5200 million. Significantly, the new insurance is backdated to November 1, or 20 days before *the catastrophic blaze.*

We believe that the incentives described above help to explain the purchase of retroactive liability coverage by MGM Grand. By retroactivist' increasing the coverage limit, MGM effectively restores the normal structure of incentives, so that the insurance company's lawyers have a stronger interest in negotiating an efficient settlement.

Efficiency in Project Evaluation

Insurance companies also develop a comparative advantage in evaluating safety projects. As a simple illustration, insurance companies that sell boiler insurance also—as would be expected—provide inspection services,

These inspections require a highly specialized engineer to inspect the boiler and its component parts. Although the company could obtain these services through an independent consultant, insurance companies are generally better suited for the task. And by agreeing to indemnify the firm for any losses, the insurance company, in effect, guarantees the quality of the inspection. This combining of insurance and inspection services provides the strongest incentive for the inspector to do a careful job.

To minimize property and casualty losses, insurance companies also generally prescribe safety projects. Such projects, of courses impose additional costs on the insured company But a competitive market for insurance effectively restrains insurers from over-prescribing safety projects. At the same time, of course, those insurance companies which systematically under-prescribe such projects will not long survive the effects of continuing higher indemnity payments. In short, a competitive marked provides insurance companies with the incentive to prescribe what should be the optimal level (based on expectations, of course, and not hindsight) of safety and maintenance investment for the insured and the insurer alike.

Besides maintaining a comparative advantage in prescribing the proper level of loss prevention measures, insurance contracts also simplify the insured company's project choice decisions by quoting a schedule of premiums associated with various levels of loss prevention. With insurance, the insured company simply asks if the cost of a safety project is less than the present value of the reduction in insurance premium. If so, it should be undertaken.

Improvement of Investment Incentives.

Corporations often enter into contracts requiring the maintenance of insurance coverage. Bong covenants, for example, frequently requiring the maintenance. The conventional explanation of such requirements is that bondholders will not invest without such a provision.

We have a different explanation: namely, that in buying

an insurance policy, the company provides a different kind of assurance to lenders—one which effectively guarantees of "bonds" a set of investment decisions by the corporation which gives the bondholders more protection. Such an assurance in turn lowers the borrowing costs to the company, while also providing the best possible incentives for the company's investment in maintenance and safety projects.

However, in the case of financially distressed companies—or even those with relatively higher probabilities of someday facing financial distress—the interests of bondholders and stockholders can diverge sharply. In such cases, financial managers intent on maximizing stockholder wealth may have incentives to take actions which will reduce the value of the bonds while increasing the value of the stock. Actions that increase the variability of the firm's cash flows, e.g., undertaking riskier investment or taking on increased financial leverage, will tend to have this effect. By so increasing the variability of the company's future cash flows, management will have of course, increased the probability of both large gains and large losses. The effect of the increase in the probability of large gains benefits only the stockholders (because the bondholder's is a fixed-income claim) and the effect of the increase in the probability of large losses falls mainly on the bondholders (because stockholders are protected by limited liability.)

Consider the case of a company with a large amount of debt outstanding. Assume also that the covenants on its existing debt have not required the purchase of insurance. How do these two conditions together influence the company's decision to invest in safety projects such as, say, a sprinkler system? Our theory says that a company carrying a large enough burden of debt would actually have a rational incentive to pass up good investments—like safety projects—which reduce the expected variability of cash flows. The company's failure to undertake such investment will decrease the value of its bonds by increasing the *expected* variability of cash flows. Our theory further tells us that, in reasonably sophisticated markets, potential bondholders will anticipate such actions by management; and without the stipulation of insurance by the covenants, they will place a lower value on the bonds when they are initially sold.

By purchasing insurance, the company hedges any losses the bondholders would suffer if it did not invest in the sprinkler system, thus eliminating the bondholders' problem. But also, and perhaps more importantly, the stockholders' incentives are changed by the insurance contract, having committed itself to carry insurance, the company now will choose to undertake any investment in safety and maintenance projects that is justified by the reduction in its insurance premiums. And lenders, provided with this assurance, will require a lower rate of interest from the company. By allowing mandatory insurance to be included in the indentures companies are securing a reduction in their borrowing costs that is greater than the cost of the insurance "loading fees." For both of these reasons then, it may be in the best interest of the company and its stockholders to include some kinds of insurance coverage in its debt covenants.

Because the potential conflict of interest between bondholders and stockholders is also greater the riskier the bonds, the use of a debt covenant requiring insurance should be more valuable in riskier debt issues. For this reason, we would expect the covenants in private placements to contain more restrictive insurance provisions than those on public issues. Insurance provisions should also be employed more frequently in privately-placed than public issues because, with only a small number of parties involved, it is chapter to administer and enforce more detailed insurance requirements.

Insurance covenants are also regularly included in other corporate contracts. For example, subcontracting agreements between corporations generally include provisions requiring the subcontractor to maintain an acceptable level of insurance coverage. In the event that an independent subcontractor were sued for a liability claim, the subcontractor might renege on the contract and declare bankruptcy The subcontractor's failure to complete the project could impose large costs on the company, as well as increasing its own potential liability The purchase of insurance by the subcontractor effectively bonds thé promise that he makes not to default on the performance of his job.

In each of the aforementioned examples—claims administration, the evaluation of safety projects, and the improvement of investment incentives and guarantees—the insured company Is paying primarily for a set of services which the Insurance company offers at a lower cost than can be obtained elsewhere. The pure insurance aspect of the contract, the transference of risk, is secondary, If not completely Irrelevant.

Risk shifting within the Corporation

For large corporations with diffuse ownership, the risk aversion of the stockholders—as we argued earlier—does not provide a rational justification for the corporate purchase of insurance. Stockholders are equally capable of diversifying the kinds of risks that insurance companies are able to minimize by pooling. In the case of the closely-held company as we also suggested, the owners' risk aversion and limited ability to achieve full diversification can provide an incentive for insurance purchases.

Up to this point, we have viewed the corporation only from the perspective of its investors and owners, the bondholders and stockholders. In reality of course, the corporation is a vast network of contracts among various parties which have conflicting as well as common interests in the company In addition to bondholders and stockholders, the managers, the employees, the suppliers, and even the customers all have a vested claim and interest—a form of investment (whether of physical or human capital)—in the company's continuation as a viable economic entity Management and labour are likely to 'have a substantial investment of human capital in the company The profitability of suppliers depends partly on the fortunes of the company buying its products. And even the buying decisions of customers, both actual and potential, can be influenced by their perceptions of the company's prospects.

Like the owners of private or closely-held companies, the corporation's managers, employees, suppliers, and customers may not be able to diversify away insurable risks; and such risks, if not insured against, can affect their future payoffs under their respective contracts. Because they are also "risk-averse," these individuals will require extra compensation to bear any risk not assumed by the owners or transferred to an insurance company Employees, for example, will demand higher wages from a company where the probability of layoff is greater. Managers will demand higher salaries (or perhaps even an equity stake in the company) where the risks of failure, insolvency and financial embarrassment are great. Suppliers will be more reluctant to enter into long-term contracts with companies whose prospects are uncertain, thus making the terms of those contracts more unfavourable. And customers, concerned about the company's ability to fulfil warranty obligations or service their products in the future, may be reluctant to buy those products.

Because of the limited liability clause, the amount of risk that can be allocated to the stockholders is limited by the capital stock of the company Companies in service industries, for instance, are often thinly-capitalized. And for such companies, where the claims—and thus the risks—of managers and employees are likely to be very large relative to the claims of investors, there may he substantial benefits from shifting those risks to an insurance company To the extent that the purchase of insurance reduces the possibility of layoffs, plant closings, or even bankruptcy such corporations could—by transferring such risks to an insurance company—be providing themselves with significant reductions in required wages and salaries. To provide a simple illustration, the purchase of business interruption insurance covering the company's ordinary payroll would reduce the risk borne by employees that, say a fire will cause a plant to shut down. The justification for the purchase of insurance, in this case, is that the cost of the insurance is more than covered by the reduction in employees' extra compensation required for otherwise bearing such risks themselves.

The Tax Advantage

One of the alleged benefits of corporate insurance is that insurance premiums are tax-deductible expenses, while reserves set aside for losses by self-insuring companies are not. And though casualty losses sustained by companies which self-insure *are* tax-deductible, the conventional argument for a tax advantage from buying insurance rests on the premise that the guaranteed annual tax shield provided by premium payments is more valuable than the random tax shield provided by unforeseen future losses. This premise, in turn, seems to be based on the notion that the company can somehow exploit the time value of money by getting its tax deductions up front" instead of in the uncertain future.

In some cases, such a strategy will result in a tax advantage; that is, the losses will take place far enough in the future that the tax savings to the insuring company—compounded at the interest rate reflecting the opportunity cost of those savings—will turn out to be significantly greater than the time-adjusted value of the tax shield created by uninsured losses. It is important to recognize, however, that decisions are made in the present, and on the basis of expected future probabilities. And on this basis, there is no obvious reason to prefer the tax effects of insurance to those of self-insurance. Remember that an insurance premium incorporates an insurance company's estimate of the expected level and timing of future losses. And thus, ignoring the effect of "loading fees" (and assuming that a company's marginal tax rate would not be reduced by a large casualty loss), the *expected* tax shields from buying insurance and self-insurance are identical.

As an example of the confusion which surrounds this tax issue, let's return to the case of MGM Grand's purchase of retroactive liability coverage. According to the *Wall Street Journal* article, cited earlier:

> *...MGM Grand, meanwhile, gets a tax break by insuring, rather than assembling a being cash reserve against losses. Premiums are tax deductible as a business expense right now while casualty reserves can' be written off until claims are paid. In MGM Grand's case that could be years form now.*

It is true that by buying the retroactive insurance, MGM did get a large tax deduction; and that the tax deduction is more valuable the earlier it is used. But what this argument fails to recognize is that if MGM had chosen to self-insure, it could have earned a normal rate of return on its capital prior to the date of any settlement. There will be no reason to prefer getting the tax savings up front to retaining and investing the so-called reserves. The income earned on those reserves, on an expected value basis, should exactly offset the value of getting the tax savings up front.

There are provisions in the tax code which, by reducing the expected tax shield from self-insurance, could favour the purchase of insurance. There is a three year carry-back and a seven year carry-forward provision. If an uninsured loss exceeds the sum of the most recent four years' earnings, the additional loss must be carried forward; and if the loss exceeds the earnings over the eleven-year period, the excess casualty loss is lost. Furthermore, when a company employs the carry-back provisions, the current y ar's tax must be totally offset before any of the previous year's taxes can be used. Finally, if the uninsured loss forces the company into bankruptcy and liquidation, any loss carry-forward will be lost.

Thus, if MGM did not expect claims losses in any single year to be large enough to push the company into a lower marginal tax bracket (thus reducing the value of the random tax shield from deducting claims losses), then the *expected* values of the tax shields from insurance and self-insurance should be equal. If, however, the company did expect very large losses to fall within a given year, then there would have been a tax advantage from buying the insurance.

It is true that by buying the retroactive insurance, MGM did get a large tax deduction; and that the tax deduction is more valuable the earlier it is used. But what this argument fails to recognize is that if MGM has chosen to self-insure, it could have earned a normal rate of return on its capital prior to the date of any settlement. There will be no reason to prefer getting the tax savings up from to retaining and investing the so-called reserves. The income earned on those reserves, on an expected value basis, should exactly offset the value of getting the tax savings up front.

There are provisions in the tax code which, by reducing the expected tax shield from self-insurance, could favour the purchase of insurance. There is a three year carry-back and a seven year carry forward provision. If an uninsured loss exceeds the sum of the most recent four years' earnings, the additional loss must be carried forward; and if the loss exceeds the earnings over the eleven-year period, the excess casualty loss is lost. Furthermore, when a company employs the carry-back provisions, the current year's tax must be totally offset before any of the previous year's tax must be totally offset before any of the previous year's taxes can be used. Finally, if the uninsured loss forces the company into bankruptcy and liquidation, any loss carry-forward will be lost.

Thus, if MGM did not expect claims losses in any single year to be large enough to push the company into a lower marginal tax bracket (thus reducing the value of the random tax shield from deducting claims losses), then the *expected* values of the tax shields from insurance and self-insurance should be equal. If, however, the company did expect very large losses to fall within a given year, then there would have been a tax advantage from buying the insurance.

To the extent, then, that the magnitude of potential losses is large relative to the company's expected annual taxable earnings, the expected value of the tax shield from insurance can be greater than the random tax shield provided by uninsured losses. This conclusion would suggest that the tax advantage of buying insurance is likely to be most significant for smaller companies with less diversified operations. For large companies with geographically dispersed operations, the tax benefits of insurance should not be important. (We would not expect Hertz to purchase collision insurance for tax purposes either). Finally, because uninsured losses do provide a (random) tax shield, companies which have other tax shields (e.g.., investment tax credits, high interest expense) would be expected to buy more insurance because of the reduced value of the expected tax deductions from self-insurance.

Regulated Companies : A Special Case

The prices of the products or services of regulated companies are established by regulatory commissions with the intention of allowing those companies to earn a "fair" rate of return for their stockholders. At the risk of oversimplifying the rate regulation process, regulators set prices which are expected to generate revenues covering the sum of expected costs, taxes, depreciation, plus a normal rate of return on the rate base. Insurance premiums are allowed as part of expected costs. If a regulated company does not insure against a particular hazard, in order for it to earn a "fair" rate of return for its stockholders, the rate commission (or the company itself) must include an expected loss estimate in computing expected costs; and this expected cost figure used in establishing allowed revenues and prices must accurately reflect the probability and magnitude of potential uninsured losses. As the rate-setting is currently administered, however, such expected costs from uninsured losses are not allowed.

Also, because uninsured casualty or liability losses are insurable risks, the regulators—like the stock market itself—would not compensate an uninsured, regulated company for bearing such risks by allowing them a higher return on its equity base.

This regulatory process provides incentives for regulated companies to buy insurance. First, because regulated companies are allowed revenues to cover the cost of expected losses *only* if they insure, they have a strong incentive to insure against all insurable risks. Second, the "loading fees" (the insurance company's expected profit after paying indemnities and providing associated services) reflected in the premiums are costs which are shifted by the regulatory process from the firm's owners to its customers. In an unregulated, competitive industry where output prices and revenues are determined in the market—regardless of whether an individual company insures—insurance loading fees cannot be passed on to the consumer." Third, because of its specialization, an insurance company is expected to have a comparative advantage in assessing the amount of expected losses. Regulators, in effect, "subcontract" this assessment by having the insurance company reflect its assessment of expected losses in the insurance premium. For all of the above reasons, we would expect a regulated company to buy significantly more insurance than a comparable, but unregulated company

Compulsory Insurance Laws

Some forms of corporate insurance coverage are required by law. Workmen's compensation laws have been enacted in every state in the U.S. These laws essentially impose on employers the responsibility of providing no-fault insurance to their workers for job-related accidents. Although self-insurance is allowed in all but five states, to qualify for self-insurance under the law, the firm must demonstrate that it has sufficient size and diversification of risks. Some states (Massachusetts, New York and North Carolina) have adopted compulsory liability insurance statutes which require some companies to purchase insurance policies. Such regulation also has the effect of increasing the likelihood that other companies will buy insurance to protect themselves against the specific hazards addressed in those regulations.

Conclusion

Our purpose in this article has been to identify and

analyze a set of incentives which justify the purchase of insurance by corporations. In so doing, we have provided a theory which attempts to explain, first, why large, widely-held companies should *not* insure against some risks; and second, why they *should* insure against others.

We believe the majority of corporations are probably making the right insurance decisions; but perhaps, in many cases, for the wrong reasons. By asking the right questions, by focusing on the important issues, corporate managers can make fewer and less expensive mistakes.

The value of any theory lies, of course, in the strength of its correspondence with events we can observe in the 'real world"; that is, in its ability to explain why things are being done as they are, and to predict how they will be done in the future. We think that our theory besides being more consistent internally, does a better job of explaining recent developments in the insurance industry than the rationale for corporate insurance that has prevailed in the insurance literature.

Industry observers have noted a pronounced tendency toward corporate self-insurance. This trend has taken several form; the increasing use of "claims only" policies, the creation of captive insurance companies, and the use of higher deductibles. In each of these developments, corporations are not using insurance to transfer risk from their investors to the insurer—as the conventional explanation holds—but for other reasons: for special insurance services like claims administration; for tax benefits (as in the formation of offshore insurance captives); and to provide assurances (in the case of stop loss" contracts with higher deductibles) not so much to instestors as to employees, managers, and suppliers—that very large property and casuality losses will not threaten the solvency of the company, or the continuity of its operations.

Part of this corporate trend toward self-insurance can be attributed to companies' increasing awareness of their ability to pool their own risks and average expected losses. Arid this, as we said earlier, is consistent with the conventional explanation of the corporate demand for insurance. We stispect, however, that another part of this movement reflects decisions, using an increasingly sophisticated framework for risk management, to all cost Companies' investors to bear insurable corporate risks themselves. In making such decisions on the correct basis (that is, except in special cases, from the point of view of well-diversified stockholders and bondholders), risk managers will be consorting corporate cash which can be put to better uses.

How can we summarize the implications of our theory for corporate risk management? All risks should not be insured, even though the owners (if the company, the stockholders and bondholders, are individually risk averse. The fact that investors have access to capital markets and the ability and incentive to diversify their portfolio holdings can make the corporate purchase of insurance a waste of stockholder funds. Insurance companies, as we have seen, may have an advantage in providing certain kinds of claims services. There also may be tax benefits, though these mast' have been exaggerated because of a failure to focus on companies *expected* tax liabilities.

In deciding whether to purchase insurance, it may also be important to focus on the set of contracts through which stockholders, bondholders, customers, suppliers, managers, employees and insurers interact. Some insurance contracts may help remedy a possible conflict of interest between bondholders and stockholders, especially in the case of companies with higher-risk investments and highly levered capital structures. Others may be valuable to the company by transferring risks away from managers, employees, and suppliers—groups which are at a relative disadvantage in bearing some insurable corporate risks. These solutions cannot, of course, be used indiscriminately, but must be applied carefully to specific corporate situations.

7

Managing Interest Rate Risk

Introduction

The sharp increase in the volatility of interest rates over the past few years has created a relatively new concern for financial executive: "interest rate risk". Since the beginning of the floating exchange rate regime, American multi-nationals have attempted to manage the risk of foreign currency fluctuations by hedging in forward markets. And, in an analogous development, serious attention is now being paid to managing corporate exposure to changes in interest rates.

In response to this unprecedented (in the U.S.) interest rate volatility, new financial markets are developing to reduce substantially the costs of shifting among parties the risk associated with interest rate changes. Interest rate futures, despite their brief history, have already become well-established financial instruments in a complex, rapidly evolving market. Financial options will soon be available.

There are number of misconceptions about the hedging assurance actually provided by interest rate futures. But when properly used, financial futures (and Options) can help some companies to maintain their operating and financing flexibility by insulating them from the adverse effects of interest rate changes. To be effective in managing interest rate risk, however, the use of financial futures and options must be part of a carefully thought out, corporate-wide financing strategy.

The first step in dealing with "interest rate risk" is to place it in its proper economic and corporate perspectives. Specifically, we want to work toward (1) a definition of interest rate risk, and (2) a general risk management framework both to assess the company's exposure to such risk, and to determine whether this risk should be managed at all. The purpose of the introductory sections is to establish that, for most non-financial corporations, the management of interest rate risk should be a "residual" strategy. That is, it should be integrated with, and subordinated to, management's longer-run financial planning.

After considering the broader questions of what interest rate risk is, and whether it should be actively managed, we then turn to an investigation of financial futures and options, evaluating their usefulness as tools for hedging corporate exposure to such risk.

Interest Rate Risk and Corporate Finance

Interest Rate Risk and Inflation risk

Interest rate risk is most commonly thought of as the potential for losses caused by changes in interest rates when funding long-term investment with shorter-term borrowings, or vice-versa. As many financial institutions have learned through experience, unanticipated movements in interest rates can result in large portfolio losses (and gains) when a portfolio of assets and liabilities is "mismatched" across maturities. The savings and loan industry, traditionally using short-term borrowings to finance long-term mortgages, offers a classic (if extreme) illustration of interest rate risk. When interest rates rose unexpectedly, financing costs rose while asset values declined, squeezing cash flow and severely decreasing net worth.

It is important to recognize, however, that the gains and losses from movements in interest rates represent only the "arithmetic" of interest rate risk. That is, the heightened variability of interest rates is really only a symptom of more fundamental developments in the economy The corporate treasurer can devise ad hoc short-run strategies that attempt to deal directly with the symptoms, while ignoring the causes. But, a more enlightened approach to the problem—one which can be incorporated into a systematic, long-range financial planning process—would be grounded in an understanding of the underlying determinants of "interest rate risk."

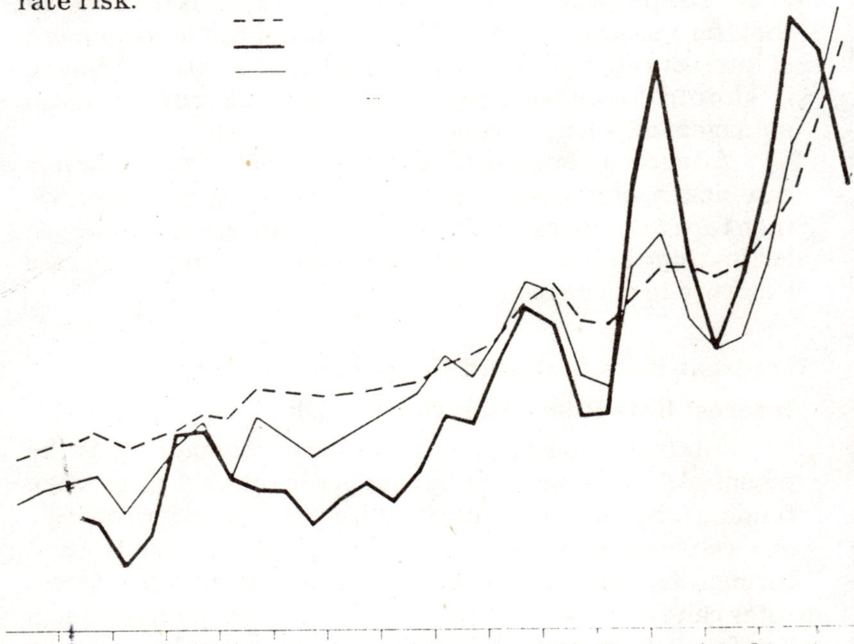

Fig 1. Interest Rates Track Inflation Over Long Run

It is an economic commonplace that changes in interest rates are strongly correlated, at least over long periods of time, with changes in inflation. If, for example, everyone knew with certainty that inflation would be ten percent per year forever, then all interest rates would incorporate a ten percent inflation "premium" in addition to a relatively constant real rate of interest. Investors would demand the premium because the principal would be repaid at a later date in money depreciated by inflated prices. Borrowers would pay the premium because they would benefit from using the funds now and repaying later in cheaper dollars.

In the real world, of course, inflation expectations are not held with certainty, and substantial forecasting errors are the norm. But, in the long-run, say decade by decade, the predicted relationship between interest and inflation rates provides a good working approximation of economic reality As shown by Figure 1, interest and inflation rates in the 1950s were both at relatively low levels, and rose in tandem in the 60's and 70's. There were, to he sure, some unpredictable lags in the adjustment of interest rates to inflation in the process of moving from the low-inflation 1950's to the high-inflation 1970's. The general relationship, however, is clearly borne out by our own experience. And the experience of the U.S. is not uncommon. High inflation countries are uniformly high interest rate countries. This means that, over the long run, the risk associated with sustained high interest rates is nothing more than the risk of sustained high inflation.

Before considering "interest rate risk," then, management should attempt to assess its exposure to "inflation risk." Because the problems of interest rate risk" and "inflation risk" are intertwined, they will have to be managed together. But the appropriate first step in dealing with "interest rate risk" is to determine the long-run exposure of the firm to changes in the rate of inflation. This assessment should allow management to choose a long-term debt structure which offsets that risk.

As Brad Cornell demonstrated in the first issue of this journal, the choice between fixed-rate and floating-rate debt should be a conscious strategic decision reflecting management's approach to "inflation risk." Floating-rate debt means, of course, higher interest payments during periods of rising inflation. And, for those companies whose real earnings are hurt by increases in inflation, long-term fixed rate debt provides a better hedge against "inflation risk," matching lower real interest costs with lower real profits in an inflationary environment. But, for companies whose long-run operating profitability keeps pace with inflation, higher inflation will also mean higher revenues to offset this increase in financing costs. For such companies, fixed-rate debt effectively increases the exposure to inflation risk, providing a windfall gain to the corporate borrower when earnings increase with rising inflation, and an unexpected loss when the rate of inflation and revenue growth slows.

Thus, while fixed-rate debt may appear to eliminate interest rate risk by fixing interest payments, it actually represents a bet on inflation—an exposure to "inflation risk." Floating-rate debt, by contrast, offers a long-run hedge against inflation risk, even though nominal interest payments will fluctuate. The real or inflation-adjusted interest rate on floating-rate debt is really fixed, while the real interest rate on fixed-rate debt floats. And, for long-range financial planning, the relative certainty about the company's real interest costs provided by the use of floating-rate debt may override all other considerations.

In the short-run, however, the relation of interest rates to observed rates of inflation is extremely variable and thus unpredictable. The reasons for this are two-fold. First, the relevant relationship is that between interest rates and *expected*, not actual, rates of inflation. Because the inflationary expectations built into interest rates can change abruptly and because they often prove to be wrong, the short-run association between interest rates and inflation is much weaker than the long-run average. Second, short-run interest rates can be significantly affected by changes in monetary and fiscal policy; and these effects can register well before the inflationary implications of the new policies are reflected in the price level. The important implication is that in the short run, which can be viewed as anywhere between, say, one day and three years, "interest rate risk" may not be directly related to "inflation risk." Consequently, even for those companies whose operations provide a natural hedge against inflation, floating-rate debt may not provide a sufficient hedge against interest rate risk.

Corporate Finance Perspectives

Let's begin by considering the problem from the perspective of the treasurer of a large, mature industrial company, with a demonstrated ability to maintain its average real profitability over inflationary and business cycles. Having first attempted to assess and limit the company's long-run exposure to inflation risk, the treasurer must then determine whether the remaining interest rate risk should be hedged. Once we assume the aim of corporate management is to maximize shareholder wealth, the question reduces to whether actively managing interest rate risk will help he shareholders achieve a higher return on their investment for bearing a given level of risk.

Finance theory maintains that, in general, managing corporate risks which would otherwise increase the expected variability (as opposed to the level) of a company's earnings does not benefit shareholders. Most company specific risks, provided they do not significantly raise the possibility of bankruptcy can be managed more efficiently by the shareholders through portfolio diversification. By pooling many different individual risks, the shareholder is protected against a major calamity affecting a particular company or industry.

To the extent that interest rate volatility represents a systematic, economy-wide phenomenon which cannot be eliminated by investors' diversification, there may be some value to shareholders in management's reducing exposure to short-run deviations from the interest rate-inflation parity. In the main, however, the management of interest rate risk should *not* be designed simply to "smooth" small fluctuations in earnings. Nor should it attempt to hedge the exposure of *financial* assets only without placing such exposure within the context of the total, corporate-wide sensitivity to interest rate changes.

Its principal aim should instead be to offset the risk that wide swings in rates will endanger the financing and operating flexibility of the company If the risk is so large that a wrong "bet" on interest rates leads to bankruptcy or to a major alteration of the business plan, then it makes sense to establish an active hedging programme to minimize that risk. If the company's interest rate risk is not of this order, then a more passive strategy involving perhaps a periodic monitoring of the overall corporate exposure, is probably sufficient.

Assessing Interest Rate Risk

To illustrate this point, consider the case of a well-capitalized, multi-national company borrowing short-term funds in many of the world's money markets. Such a firm is likely to have a revenue/cost performance record which tracks inflation fairly well over, say a five-year cycle. Although inflation and interest rate risks are not managed directly, the long-term risk that abrupt changes in inflation or interest rates will lead to financial distress is very small. At any given time, the company will be taking many small, partly offsetting bets on inflation and interest rates (and on exchange rates as well), which when aggregated over time and viewed in relation to the capitalization of the company result in a low risk profile. A large firm can weather a good number of individually adverse outcomes without unduly harming its operations. To extend the gambling analogy the player placing a large number of bets (of roughly the same size) expects to lose a few, but these are likely to be offset by other bets.

Consider also, however, a smaller growth company with narrowly-concentrated operations, and with a more uncertain relationship between real profitability and inflation. Because individual financing decisions can have a major impact on the overall company, management does not get the benefit of taking many potentially offsetting bets. In this case, a sharp swing in interest rates could do severe damage to the company's operating cash flow, impairing its ability to raise capital and carry out its business plan. Such a company may have a very large exposure to interest rate risk—an exposure which should probably be managed directly.

Having established the need to reduce this exposure, the corporate strategist will then want to consider the use of financial futures and options. The next several sections provide an introduction to these new financial instruments, dispel some common misconceptions, and evaluate their relative merits as tools for managing interest rate risk.

FINANCIAL FUTURES

Basic Concepts

Like commodities futures, financial futures contracts are agreements by which two parties set a 'rice today for a transaction that will not be completed until a specified date in the future. For example, consider a futures contract for $1 million on 90-day Treasury bills, deliverable in six months, and 'priced at 88.00 (based on 100.00 being par), for annualized discount of 12.00 percent. These terms 'bilge the seller of the futures contract to deliver a 1 million 90-day Treasury bill to the buyer on the specified date, six months in the future, for the price set today, 88.00.

At the end of the six months, the prevailing discount on 90-day Treasury bills is not likely to be exactly 12.00 percent, and one party will make a profit—and the other party a loss—equal to the difference between the actual (spot) price and the price set six months previously. The buyer of the futures contract will profit if interest rates decline below the rate set by the contract (or, equivalently, if prices rise above the price set by the contract), while the seller stands to gain if interest rates rise and prices fall below the value set by the contract. As illustrated in Figures 6.1 and 6.2 (page 133), the gains and losses are "symmetric," which is to say that the buyer's gains are the seller's losses, and vice versa. (In fact, these gains or losses are paid along the way, and not at the end of the contract. This is the "mark-to-market" feature the futures instrument, which will be discussed later).

As Table 1 indicates, futures contracts are now available on a variety of government, as well as a few private market, debt instruments. Currently, the most widely accepted contracts, as gauged by market liquidity, are those on government issues.

Table 1 : Currently Popular Futures Contracts

Contract	Principal	Open Interest* (March 1982)
90-Day Treasury Bills	$ 1,000,000	38,000
90-Day bank CDs	1,000,000	10,000
90-Day Eurodollar TDs**	1,000,000	5,000
GNMAs	100,000	65,000
20-Year Treasury Bonds	100,000	180,000

One possible corporate use of financial futures is to convert a floating-rate loan into a synthetic fixed-rate loan. For example, the borrower of a 90-day floating-rate Eurodollar loan could use the Eurodollar futures market to "lock in" his interest rate for the next rollover date. That is, assuming a $1 million loan is scheduled for repricing in June, the borrower could sell in March a $1 million 90-day Eurodollar CDs futures contract, promising to take delivery in June. If interest rates rise, the higher interest payments will be offset by an equal gain on the futures contract. If interest rates decline, however, the benefit of lower interest payments for the June quarter will be offset by an equal loss on the futures contract (as the price of the contract will have increased). By tinsing interest rate futures to fix" a floating—rate loan, the borrower in effect eliminates the risk of higher interest payments; but he also gives up the chance to gain from an interest rate decline.

This is the essence of the financial futures market:

trading interest rate risks. A hedge exists only when one party has a risk somewhere in his portfolio that he can offset with a futures market contract, but this means trading away the opportunity for gain as well as the potential for loss.

The Yield Curve

The relationship between current interest rates and the rates built into the corresponding futures contracts depends on the shape of the yield curve. Recall that the shape of the yield curve reflects the rates of interest paid on progressively longer maturities of the same financial instrument. The yield curve thus embodies investors' expectations about the future direction of interest rates. A sharply upward—sloping yield curve, in which yields on longer maturities are considerably higher than those on shorter maturities, reflects the market consensus that rates are more like lst' to rise in the future. An "inverted" yield curve, by contrast, means that rates are expected to fall.

Thus, whether the futures market offers an interest rate for a future period that is less than, equal to, or greater than today's rate on the same financial instrument is determined largely by those expectations embodied in the shield curve, The following example should help explain why.

Investors are always offered a choice, say, between (1) buying :in 90—day Treasury bill today and rolling it over into another 90—day Treasury bill in three months; or (2) buying a 180-day Treasury bill today. If the investor takes the first option (rolling over successive 90—day bills), then his total six-month return is uncertain. But, if he also locks in a return on the 90—day T—bill he plans to buy in three months (by buying a T—bill futures contract), then his six month return on the transaction becomes certain. This means that he can compare the return on the rollover option in combination with the futures position to the return on simply buying a six month T—bill.

Because both returns are certain, investors facing this choice will always choose the option offering the higher return. This process (known as "arbitrage" of comparing returns, and electing the alternative promising the higher return, guarantees that the futures market rate will reflect the expectations embodied in the yield curve of the underlying financial instrument. In this example, the arbitrage process ensures that if six month T-bills are yielding considerably less than three month T-bills, then the 90 day T-bll futures rate (net of tax and liquidity considerations) will be below the current spot 90 day T-bill rate.

Because the futures markets are constantly arbitraged against the existing "cash" markets by the major financial institutions around the world, the rates and prices offered in the futures market bear a strong resemblance to the rates in the financial, or cash, markets. If they did not, then these institutions would be foregoing riskless profit opportunities —a situation which is not likely to last for any appreciable length of time. The result, as suggested, is that the futures prices (and hence interest rates) for the different contract maturities of short-term instruments like T—bills and Eurodollars will closely reflect the shape of the yield curve on those instruments.

For example, if the yield curve for Eurodollar rates is inverted, the futures market will reflect this inversion by setting the interest rate on the contracts deliverable in three months higher (by setting the price lower) than the rates on the contract due in six or nine months. This means that futures do not allow the investor or the borrower to lock in today's interest rate. As the above example illustrates, one can lock in only the rate offered by the market, which will necessarily reflect the shape of the yield curve.

The futures market thus offers insurance to borrowers only against *unexpected* changes in interest rates. When the yield curve is sharply upward sloping, and interest rates are thus expected to rise, the financial manager will be able to lock in only the higher interest rate expected by the futures market. Hence, the borrower will be protected only against increases in interest rates above those already impounded into the current yield curve.

Table 2 : Basis Risk: CD Futures vs. CD Cash

	90-Day CD Rate, Secondary Market		Futures Rate on March 1982 Bank CD Contract	
Date	**Rate (Percent)**	**Change from 11/9/81 (Basis Points)**	**Rate (Percent)**	**Change from 11/9/81 (Basis Points)**
11/09/81	13.00	—	13.14	—
01/05/82	13.00	0	14.15	+ 101
01/20/82	13.85	+ 85	15.05	+ 191

It is also important to remember that the shape of the yield curve can change, even when spot interest rates do not. That is, because the market may change its expectations about future interest rates during the period covered by a given futures contract, rolling over a series of short-term futures contracts to hedge a longer-term commitment does not provide the equivalent of a fixed-rate commitment. When the roll-over date arrives, the company will be able to lock in only the then current futures market rate, not the rates that prevailed at the time of the original hedge. Thus, rolling over futures contracts to hedge a floating-rate loan will not protect the borrower (beyond the period covered by the contract already in effect) from a sudden upward shift in interest rate expectations that takes place while the contract is in effect. Furthermore, because the futures markets offer contracts with at most two-year maturities, this "rollover risk" means that futures cannot be used to hedge for the longer-term planning horizon.

The futures-to-yield curve relationship also means that use of the futures market cannot provide the borrower with cheaper financing costs, or the lender with a higher expected return, than what is currently available in the financial markets. When a borrower uses futures to convert a three-month floating-rate loan into a one-year fixed-rate obligation, the synthetic fixed rate of interest paid will not end up differing greatly from the rate on one-year debt instruments. Not surprisingly, there is no free lunch in the futures market.

The Margin Account

To purchase a futures contract, the buyer does not pay cash for the full or partial value of the underlying investment. Only a small cash outlay, called the "margin requirement," is necessary The investor is obliged to maintain a minimum amount in a margin "account" throughout the life of the contract as a kind of good faith assurance that all future commitments under the terms of the contract will be met. Any amounts over this level may be withdrawn and invested. But, if a fall in the price of the futures position causes the value of the account to fall below the minimum level, additional cash must be deposited. Brokerage firms often pay interest (this is negotiable) on margin accounts, so that these are not, strictly speaking, idle funds.

Cash Flows and the Mark-to-Market Feature

A feature of futures markets that can make otherwise perfect hedges substantially less than perfect in the eyes of corporate treasurers is the "mark-to-market" requirement. The value of an interest rate futures contract reflects, of course, the expected yield on the underlying financial instrument when the contract expires. As expectations shift, spot interest rates change, the shape of the entire yield curve may change, and thus the value of futures contracts change. This happens continuously At the close of each day's trading, futures exchanges mark all accounts to their current market value, debiting the losers' and crediting the winners' margin accounts in cash.

As can be imagined, the balance in the margin account may fluctuate widely during the term of the contract. So, even while use of the futures market can lock in a particular interest rate over a period of time, the daily mark-to-market feature makes the actual timing of the holder's cash inflows and our-flows highly unpredictable over that same period.

For instance, consider the strategy of using T-bill contracts to transform a floating-rate loan of $10 million into a one-year fixed rate loan. The procedure would be to sell ten three-month futures, ten six-month futures, and ten nine-month futures contracts. The interest rate on the initial three month period would he determined by the prevailing spot rare, but each successive three month period can be locked in by buying this "strip" of futures contracts. Over time the futures positions will be "unwound" and the gains (losses) on futures will offset the higher (lower) interest rate pavements for the three month period in question. At least, that is what happens in principle.

More likely, the actual cash flows, while offsetting on a cumulative basis by the *end* of the year, will follow an unpredictable pattern *during* that year. Suppose after two months the entire yield curve shifts upward by 100 basis points. Then all of the futures contracts will increase in value by $2,500 each; or on the 30 contracts, by $75,000. This is cash credited to the hedger's account which, if interest rates do not shift again, will compensate for the higher interest payments to be made over the next 10 months.

But if interest rates decline across the yield curve by 100 basis points after the first two months, the company would suffer a *loss of* $75,000 on the 30 futures positions. While this loss will eventually be offset by lower interest payments over the next 10 months, the uncertain pattern of cash flows makes even short-term cash management somewhat problematic.

Unfortunately, in hedging with financial futures, it is not only the timing of cash flows that is uncertain, but often the cumulative outcome as well. The examples offered up to this point may have given the impression that financial futures will completely insulate the user against specific interest rate risks. In moving from the basic theoretical concepts to the practical management of interest rate risk, however, I want to impress on the reader that most actual hedging situations will not match the textbook cases presented so far. Or, now for the bad news.

Futures Provide Rather Less Than Perfect Hedges

Basis Risk

Assuming that management has first correctly assessed its real economic exposure to changes in interest rates, there still remains another serious pitfall in hedging with financial futures. The spread between the interest rates on the instrument being hedged, and on the instrument doing the hedging (the futures contract) may not be stable. This interest rate spread is called the basis,' and uncertainty about this spread is known as basis risk."

If, for instance, a borrower wants to convert a prime-based bank loan into a synthetic fixed-rate loan using 90-day T-bill futures, then any *changes* in the spread between the T-bill rate and the prime rate will make the conversion less than perfect. If the prime and T-bill rates do not move in lock-step, the relationship between T-bill rates and prime will shift. This means that the hedger may still suffer economic losses (or enjoy unexpected gains) due to interest rate fluctuations. For certain combinations of financial instruments, this risk of a change in the basis" can be substantial.

The only short-term futures market instrument offering substantial liquidity as far forward as 18 months is the 90-day Treasury bill contract. Mainly for this reason, T-bill futures are commonly used to hedge floating-rate bank loans tied to prime. In view of the historical relationship between prime and three-month T-bill rates, basis risk should be cause for some concern.

To help illustrate the magnitude of the basis risk problem, Figure 2 presents the quarterly average interest rates for both 90-day Treasury bills and bank prime rates from 1970 through 1981. Figure 3 shows the spread between the quarterly average rates, thus providing a longer-run view of the basis risk involved. From these charts, it is clear that although the rates do move in a roughly synchronous

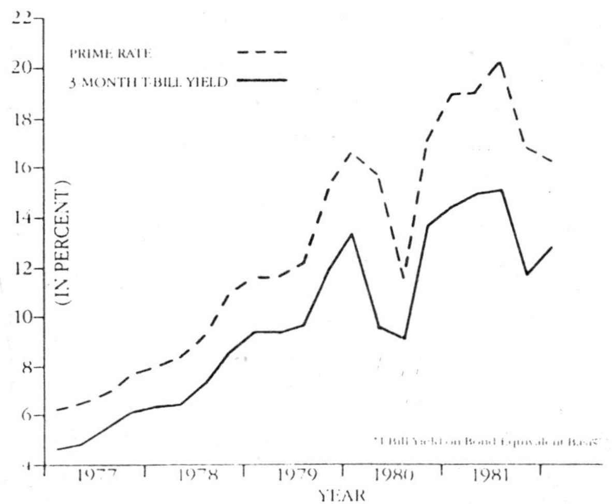

Fig. 2 : Prime Rate vs. 3-Month T-BiII Yield* (Quarterl ·)

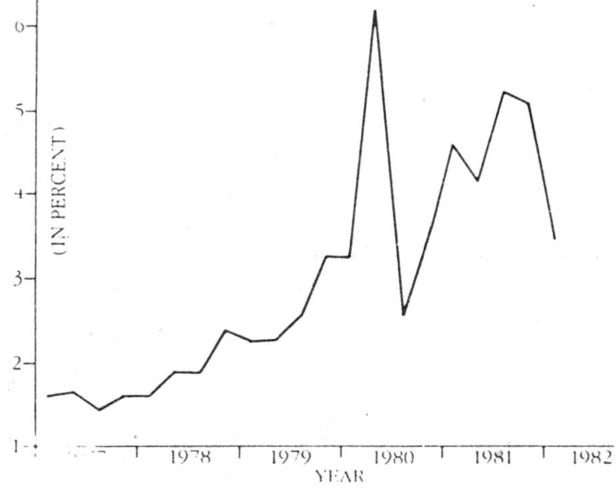

Fig. 3 : Prime Rate vs. 3-Month T-Bill Yield (Quarterl · Spread)

manner, the spread or basis has been highly variable since late 1979. The general increase in the volatility of interest rates has also made the spreads between interest rates on different short-term financial instruments considerably less stable. The effectiveness of T-bills as a vehicle for hedging prime rate loans has therefore been substantially reduced, just when the need for such a vehicle has dramatically increased.

Even these exhibits tend to understate toe problem of basis risk. In the actual process of setting a hedge, the transaction is completed over a very short period—a day or probably at most a week, depending on the size of the hedge. This means that the hedger is effectively locking in an interest rate spread between prime and the T-bills futures rate which mast' not be representative of the long-run average relationship between rates. Instead, the particular spread locked in may be a short-term aberration. And even though this spread does not reflect the long-run average, it nevertheless becomes—purely by an accident of timing—the relevant basis for the borrower. Thus, the average basis risk over a quarter may not reflect the actual basis risk associated with a prime-T-bill hedge that is' transacted over the much shorter period of time.

Figures 4 and 5 are thus included to show the spread between T-bills and bank prime over a month and a week, respectively Consider the effect of setting a hedge at point "A" (February 1980) on Figure 5' Hedging with a 90-day T-bills futures contract would have subjected the prime rate borrower to a basis fluctuation of about 700 basis points (the other extreme is the spike at point "B," mid-April 1980)- Over a full year the basis is more stable. But, even 50), the spread was still some 150 basis points higher in February 1981 (point "C") than it was a year earlier. This means that a prime-rate borrower hedging a loan over this period with T-bill futures would have experienced a substantial loss due to the shift in the basis.

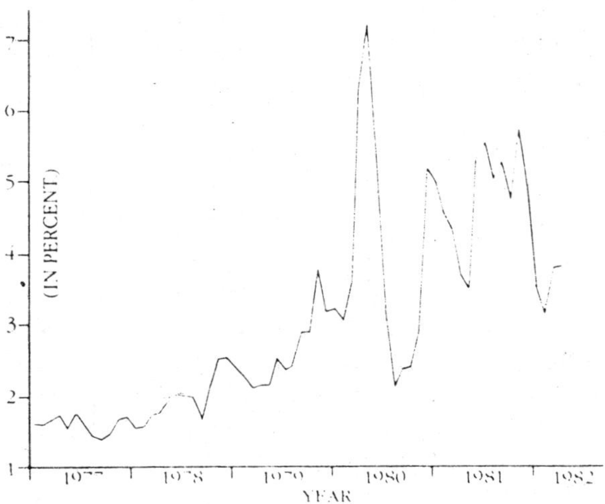

Fig. 4 : Prime Rate vs. 3-Month T-Bill Yield (Monthly Spread)

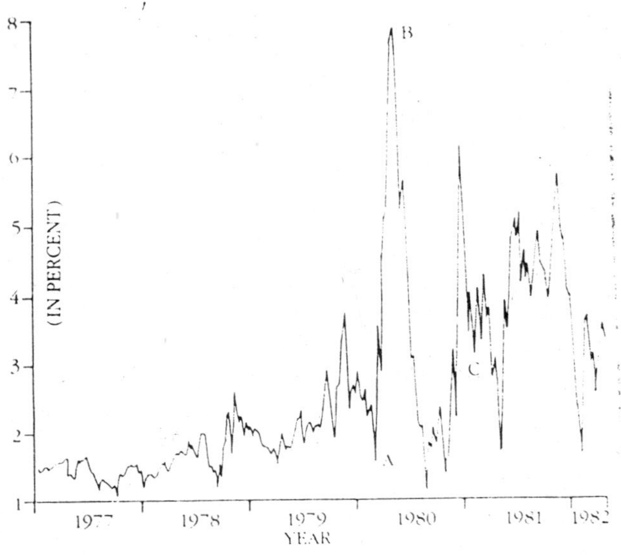

Fig. 5 : Prime Rate vs. 3-Month T-Bill Yield (Weekly Spread)

The most sensible approach to minimizing basis risk is to use the futures instrument whose interest rate moves most closely in tandem with the debt instrument being hedged. While the list of futures contracts available is still quite short, one good example is the use of Eurodollar futures to hedge a Eurodollar loan. This significantly reduces the kind of basis risk addressed above. The Eurodollar futures market, however, is still much less liquid than futures contracts on U.S. government securities.

And, even in this case, basis risk in not entirely eliminated. While one might think that interest rate changes on the underlying Eurodollar loan and the Eurodollar futures contract would be more or less the same, this is not always so. In the example that appears in Table 2, the interest rates on bank Certificates of Deposit (CDs) in the cash or "spot" market are compared to rates in the CDs futures market. In November 1981 90-day bank CDs were yielding 13 percent, while the March 1982, when the CD rate was again at 13 percent (a net change of zero basis points), the same March futures contract had increased by 101 basis points to 14.15 percent. By March the rate on the futures contract would have converged with the interest rate prevailing in the cash market, because the contract specifies delivery of the cash instrument. The hedger's risk, however, would have been that the loan had to be repriced in the interim period. For example, if the repricing was scheduled for January 1982, the hedger would have gained or lost (depending on the position taken) from this fluctuation in the basis. Thus, a surprising amount of basis risk exists even when using a futures contract on the same underlying instrument as the one being hedged.

The problems of basis risk are sometimes reduced by the use of more complex futures strategies involving multiple contracts across instruments and maturities. This can provide a synthetic futures instrument that fits the underlying instrument more closely than just a T-bill or T-bond contract. These strategies are worthy of case-by-case study, particularly if the basis risk problem seems severe, but are too specific for consideration here.

In summary, basis risk must be carefully assessed before hedging transactions are undertaken. Using futures as a hedging device will always entail some basis risk. In some cases, it will be substantial. Consequently, the effective use of financial futures requires some knowledge of the relationships between rates on a variety of instruments.

Accounting vs. Economic Risk

Another pitfall for the hedger lies in the corporate accounting practice of recording assets and liabilities at historical instead of market values. Gains or losses are generally realized by accountants only when assets are sold or liabilities retired. And as a result, a company's economic exposure to interest rate variability can be quite different from its balance sheet exposure.

The stock market, as the accumulating evidence suggests, sees through accounting fictions, pricing companies according to the economic or market value of their assets and liabilities. The management of financial risks should, therefore, attempt to manage real economic, not illusory accounting exposures.

If exposure to interest rate risk is assessed on the basis of book values, and if book values exceed market values, then management may tend to over-hedge its actual exposure. "Over-hedging," however, is a misnomer when using financial futures. The symmetry of futures gains and losses means that when one "over-hedges" with futures, one has actually switched to the other side of the bet.

To see this more clearly, suppose a company purchased $10 million of bonds in the mid-1970's at par with a 9 percent coupon and, facing higher current yields, wanted to protect those bonds against a further loss of value from even higher interest rates. The company should not sell $10 million of futures contracts if the bonds have actually declined in value by $3 million. Only the current market value of $7 million should be hedged. The $3 million is gone, and the futures markets cannot retrieve lost opportunities. By hedging the face value of $10 million, management would actually be taking a *speculative* position in the opposite direction; that is, instead of merely hedging against higher interest rates, management would in effect be gambling on rates to move higher.

Futures and Options

Options are More Flexible

Markets for buying and selling options contracts on financial instruments are expected to be available in the near future. They will be similar to financial futures in their selection of underlying financial instruments: namely, government debt contracts. They will also provide a hedging alternative which will minimize or even eliminate two problems of hedging with futures :

(1) the uncertainty about the timing of cash flows resulting from their mark-to-market feature; and
(2) the possibility of taking a large speculative position when over-hedging.

A borrower wanting protection from rising interest rates can buy put" options on government debt, which will appreciate as the prices of government issues fall. The put option gives the holder the right to *sell* the underlying instrument, for a price set today any time over the life of the contract.

Investors seeking a hedge against falling rates can buy 'call" options, which will appreciate as rates fall and bond prices rise. A call option is simply the reverse of a put: it allows the holder to *buy* the underlying instrument any time up to maturity, for a price set today

In contrast to futures, there is no mark-to-market feature with an options contract and, therefore, no fluctuating margin account to be maintained. This means that the cash flow uncertainty associated with using futures is not a problem with options.

Also unlike futures, the purchase of either a put or a call option limits the buyer's loss to the price paid for the option contract (the premium). The option buyer's potential for gain, however, is unlimited. The trading of risk is thus said to be "asymmetrical." The seller (writer) of options must, however, receive fair compensation for bearing the risk others are unwilling to tolerate. Recall that unexpected interest rate swings are an economy-wide phenomenon that cannot be eliminated, only transferred (for a price) among willing market participants. In this case the seller of the financial options contract has a potential gain limited to the size of the option premium, but incurs the risk of a large, potentially unlimited loss. The fact that the seller bears more risk (relative to the futures trader) means, necessarily, that there will be a proportionately higher expected return. This means that the options premiums for insurance against adverse interest rate moves will be higher than the hedging costs associated with futures.

Nevertheless, for many companies, or for a particular situation involving a large one-time transaction, the higher cost of hedging with options may well be offset by the value of the new risk distribution, and the elimination of the cash flow uncertainty inherent in futures.

In addition, while options do not solve the basis risk problem, the asymmetry of their risk distribution means that they can be used to over-insure. In the earlier example, the company purchasing a $10 million futures contract to hedge only $7 million in bonds was said to be over-hedging, but was actually taking a speculative position in the opposite direction. In the case of options, however, hedging $10 million is still only hedging. Since the option buyer's loss is limited to the initial premium, there is no possibility of additional losses from extra contracts. Over-insuring with options simply costs a little more (i.e., a more expensive premium for the options contracts) than a perfectly matched hedge.

Using Options to Hedge Commitments

Another distinct advantage of options is the additional flexibility they can provide in hedging commitments. To illustrate this flexibility, consider the case of a bank or insurance company which commits itself to lend money in six months at a rate set today The lender could attempt to protect himself against an intervening change in rates by selling a six-month futures contract. The hedge may work if the transaction proceeds as planned. Suppose, however, the borrower walks away from his commitment to borrow the money In this case, the lender will he left holding an open futures position, exposing him to the possibility of unexpected gain or loss.

Options, however, provide protection against this uncertainty A lender can charge a commitment fee to cover the cost of buying put option contracts to hedge the interest rate exposure. If the borrower reneges on his commitment, he loses the commitment fee. The lender, while minimizing or even eliminating potential losses, will benefit from any gains from the open position.

Although options positions can be constructed to mirror futures positions, their real value rests in their asymmetric risk characteristics. Combinations of options positions allow for a wealth of strategies, specifically tailored to the risk/reward needs of a company or a particular situation.

In short, while futures and options both can provide insurance against interest rate risks, they will have different advantages, and thus will play somewhat different roles in hedging such risks. These roles will depend on such factors as the relevant risk/reward distribution desired by management, the ability of the operations to handle uncertain cash flows, and the amount of interest rate insurance required. Another consideration is that financial futures are older and more established, but financial options markets can be expected to mature rapidly

Conclusion

In response to the increased volatility of interest rates, financial institutions have been forced to monitor closely and manage actively their exposure to interest rate risk. Because the sensitivity of the value of most financial assets to changes in interest rates is fairly predictable, financial futures and options should prove especially useful in managing the asset/liability exposures of S & L's, commercial banks, investment banks, and insurance companies.

For most non-financial corporations, the effect of interest rate changes on the economic value of their assets and liabilities is more difficult to assess. Nevertheless, these companies also face risk associated with variability in inflation and interest rates; and financial managers, in many cases, should probably be reviewing this exposure in a more systematic way.

Such a review should begin by examining, and perhaps revising, the companys long-range strategic and financing policies. Because interest rates and inflation move together over long periods of time, interest rate risk is, in the the long run, nothing more than inflation risk. Long-range financial planning accordingly should concentrate on the long-term exposure of the business to changes in the rate of inflation. The effects of varying inflation rates on the company's future cash flows should be simulated, if possible, at the consolidated corporate level, to gain a broad view of the company's overall *net* exposure to interest rate, inflation, and exchange rate fluctuations. (This is meant to correct the problem—often found in large organizations-of the treasury and planning offices hedging the same risk or, perhaps even more common, hedging individual risks which if left alone would cancel each other out.)

Having once established the company's long-term exposure to changes in inflation, management should attempt to minimize that exposure by choosing an appropriate long-term debt structure. For the mature, diversified company whose earnings tend to rise and fall with inflation, this may very well be a neutral strategy employing floating-rate debt as a hedge against inflation risk. Because the long-run inflation to interest rate relationship is fairly stable, the losses and gains from short-term interest rate fluctuations tend to cancel out. Consequently a large corporation that is properly capitalized for the long haul will have the financial muscle to wait for the long-run relationship between interest rates and inflation to prevail. For such companies, attempting to hedge a modest exposure to short-run aberrations in interest rates is probably not a worthwhile exercise.

When viewed apart from the risk of inflation changes, interest rate risk is thus largely a short-run phenomenon. But, for those companies with large exposures, the short run must be managed. Where there is a large possibility that unexpected changes in interest rates can cause a sharp fall in net worth, which in turn could drastically reduce the company's financing flexibility management should give serious attention to an active hedging strategy

Financial futures and options are the tools for hedging interest rate risk. They enable management to choose, over the short run, the interest rate exposure it wants independently of its financial structure. Their use, however, is attended by a different set of problems and considerations. Several characteristics of financial futures and options deserve special attention:

- Financial futures can be used to trade interest rate risk. The user, in hedging, forfeits potential gains, but eliminates the chance of large potential losses caused by interest rate changes.
- Financial futures cannot reduce financing costs.
- Financial futures cannot provide a perfect hedge against unexpected interest rate movements.
- Interest rates on financial futures reflect the yield curve, and therefore allow the hedger to lock in only the markets' expected interest rates, not interest rates currently available in the cash market.
- Even though financial futures contracts can lock in an interest rate, the subsequent cash flow pattern will remain uncertain.
- Financial options can be used to trade risk in an asymmetric manner, allowing construction of highly complex positions.
- Financial options do not necessarily involve uncertain cash flows over the hedge period.

- Financial options can be used to over-insure, while financial futures cannot.
- Financial options can be used to hedge commitments while futures cannot.

With these considerations in mind, both financial futures and financial options can be used effectively in managing in erest rate risk. Such risk management programmes, though, do require constant evaluation and refinement, and these must be considered as part of the costs of such insurance. Further, because the markets for trading interest rate risk are still evolving and the needs for managing interest rate risk are changing, today's problems and solutions may well differ substantially from those a few years hence.

8

Evolving Market for Swaps

A recent advertisement extols swaps as 'a tool no financial manager can ignore." While this statement has the hyperbolic ring of Madison Avenue prose, it is nevertheless quite clear that the swaps market—a relatively new and rapidly developing market—has become increasingly important. As with other evolving markets in the past, there exists confusion about certain economic implications of this market, especially among some corporate treasurers to whom these instruments are being marketed. Questions that deserve consideration include: (1) How does the swaps market relate to other financial, markets? (2) How (and why) did the swaps market evolve? (3) What goes into the pricing of a swap, particularly the evaluation of credit risk? (4) What direction might the swaps market be expected to take in the future? Our paper focuses on these questions; and, in so doing, it proposes a general analytical framework that should prove helpful in evaluating both the broad variety of swaps now available, and those that are yet to be devised.

Analysis of Swap Transactions

As its name implies, a swap is normally defined as an exchange. More specifically, it is an exchange of cash flows over time between two parties (generally referred to as the "counterparties"). The first swaps developed from parallel loans arranged between two companies in different countries, a form popular in the 1970s. To illustrate a parallel loan, suppose a British company makes a loan denominated in pounds to a US company, which in turn makes a loan of equal value denominated in dollars to the British company. As illustrated in Figure 1, these loans have parallel interest and principal repayment schedules. By entering into this parallel loan agreement, the British company is able to transform a debt incurred in pounds into a fully-hedged US dollar liability. There are, however, two potentially important problems with parallel loans: (1) default by one party does not release the other from making its contractually obligated payments; (2) although the loans effectively cancel one another, they remain on-balance-sheet items for accounting and regulatory purposes. Early in the 1980s a new transaction known as a "currency swap" was devised to overcome these problems; and because of its success, it effectively displaced the use of parallel loans.

The Currency Swap : A currency swap involves the same pattern of cash flows as a parallel loan. Indeed, without any modification, Figure 1 could be used to illustrate the cash flows for a fixed currency swap where firm A pays a fixed interest rate in dollars and receives a fixed rate in pounds, while the counterparty, firm B, pays fixed-rate pounds and receives fixed-rate dollars. Alternatively, a swap transaction could be illustrated by looking at the cash flows paid and received over time by one of the counterparties. Figure 2 illustrates the position of the British firm A in this fixed currency swap.

Although a swap is defined as an "exchange" of cash flows, there need not be an actual exchange of payments. Instead, at specified intervals, only the net cash flows could be exchanged, and the party that would have received the lower of the cash flows could simply pay the other the difference in the two cash flows. In the case of currency swaps, the counterparties do exchange interest payments; however, the exchange is conditional in the sense that if one party defaults, the other is released from its obligation.

In currency swaps, moreover, the counterparties generally exchange the principals at an agreed-upon rate of exchange and then re-exchange at the end of the agreement; but this exchange also need not occur. The principal could instead be "notional," as is generally the case in interest rate swaps (which we take up later).

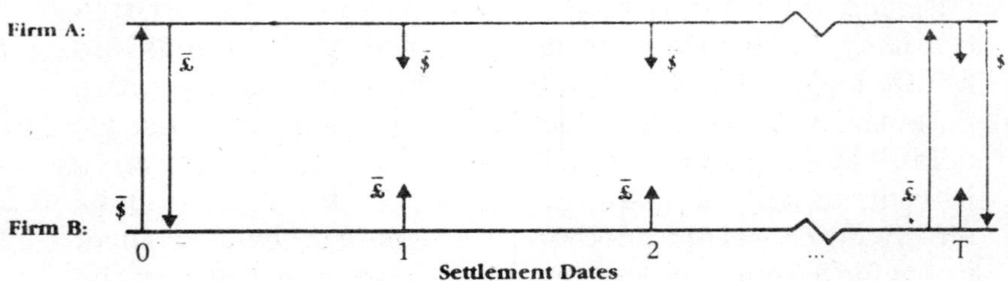

Fig. 1 : Cash Flows in a Parallel Loan Agreement.
The British firm A simultaneously horrows dollars from American firm B and loans an equivalent amount denominated in pounds to firm B at time 0. During the term of the loan, firm A makes interest payments in dollars to firm B, while firm B makes interest payments in pounds to firm A. At maturity (time T) the two firms make their final interest payments and return the principals. Firm A returns dollars and firm B returns pounds.

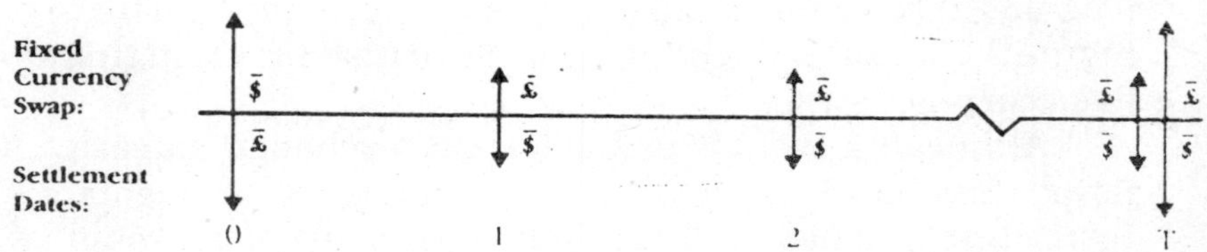

Fig. 2 : Cash Flows from a Fixed Currency Swap
The British firm A pays interest at a fixed dollar rate ($) and receives interest at a fixed pound rate (£) The long arrows denote the initial exchange of principal and the re-exchange at maturity; the short arrows denote the cash flows exchanged over the course of the agreement.

By thus converting the older parallel loan transaction into a conditional exchange of the cash flows, the currency swap reduces the probability and magnitude of default. Furthermore, as implied above, current regulatory and accounting practice treats swap contracts as off-balance-sheet items. Thus, as stated earlier, the currency swap accomplishes the goals of its predecessor, the parallel loan agreement, while eliminating the major remaining problems with that transaction.

Swaps as Packages of Forward Contracts : One of the major themes of this paper, to which we shall return throughout, is the fundamental similarity between swaps and forward contracts. In fact, it is our contention that any swap can be decomposed into a series of forward contracts.

Again consider Figure 2, which illustrates the cash flows in a fixed currency swap—one in which the firm pays fixed-rate interest in one currency and receives fixed-rate interest in another. The cash flows for the counterparty receiving pounds and paying dollars at time 1 are equivalent to those from holding a long position in pounds in a pound-dollar forward contract. This also applies to each settlement date between 2 and T; hence this currency swap for firm A is equivalent to a package of T long forward contracts in pounds. The positions are reversed for the counterparty.

We believe this decomposition of swaps into forward contracts is the most productive way of evaluating swaps, particularly the pricing of swaps. Simple swaps have been standardized and are now quoted virtually as commodities; and for such swaps this method of analysis will seem roundabout. But, as we will demonstrate, for more complicated swaps, where the timing of cash-flow exchanges differ or where the principal changes, decomposition of cash flows into forward contracts is the simplest, most effective analytical approach.

Currency Coupon Swaps : In a currency swap, as we have seen, the counterparties agree on the timing of the exchanges, the principal amounts of the currencies that will be exchanged, the interest rates (which reflect credit market forward prices) that will determine the future cash flows, and the exchange rates used to calculate the net cash flows. The earliest currency swaps were fixed currency swaps, which specified fixed interest rates in both currencies. Soon after came a variant of the fixed currency swap called the currency coupon swap. In such an arrangement, the interest rate in one currency is fixed and the other is floating.

Interest Rate Swaps : The interest rate swap, which was introduced shortly after currency swaps, is a special case of the currency coupon swap—one in which all the cash flows are denominated in a single currency. Figure 3 illustrates a simple interest rate swap. The primary difference between Figures 2 and 3 is that the exchanges of principal flows at time 0 and T net to zero because they are of the same amount and denominated in the same currency.

Basis Rate Swaps : To this point, we have described swaps in which both interest rates are fixed (fixed currency swaps) and swaps in which one interest rate is fixed and one is floating (simple interest rate swaps and currency coupon swaps). In a basis rate swap, both interest rates are floating. The primary effect of such swaps is to allow floating-rate cash flows calculated on one basis to be exchanged for floating rate cash flows calculated on another. For example, it permits firms to make conversions from one-month LIBOR to six-month LIBOR, or from LIBOR to US commercial paper rates. A basis rate swap is equivalent to pairing two simple interest rate swaps such that the flows are converted from floating to fixed, and then converted from fixed to floating (but on a different basis).

Commodity Swaps : A swap is, in effect, an exchange of net cash flows calculated to reflect changes in designated prices. So far, we have considered only two prices, interest rates and exchange rates. However, swaps defined in prices other than interest rates and foreign exchange rates are also possible. Once a principal amount is determined and that principal contractually converted to a flow, any set of forward prices can be used to calculate the cash flows (and thus the difference checks).

Consider, for example, the possibility of swaps denoted in commodities such as oil and wheat. The counterparties could agree to some notional principal and to the conversion of this principal to flows using a fixed dollar interest rate and the US price of wheat. Such a swap is analytically no different from a currency swap where forward prices of wheat replace the forward currency prices. In addition, neither firm need be in the wheat business; the difference checks are paid in dollars, not wheat. Moreover, in a swap in which the firm elects to pay with wheat, it can receive either fixed or floating rates in any currency or commodity.

Swaps with Timing Mismatches : In addition to differences resulting from the price used to calculate the cash flows (i.e., interest rates, foreign exchange rates, and commodity prices), swaps can differ in the timing of the cash flows. At the simplest level, it could be that one party is paying on a monthly basis while the other is on a quarterly schedule. More significant differences in the timing of the cash flows include so-called "zero" swaps—swaps in which one party makes no payment until maturity—and customized swaps in which the payments from one party vary, either in terms of timing or amount.

Swaps with Option-Like Payoffs : We have stressed the similarity of swaps to forward contracts. Indeed, the payoff profile for a simple swap contract is identical to that of a forward contract. Fig. 4 presents a simple case in which the firm pays a floating interest rate and receives a fixed rate. This firm has positive net cash flows when the short-term interest rate is below that existing at the contract origination date.

Swaps can also be constructed so as to have option-like provisions which limit the range of outcomes. For example, suppose that a firm with a floating-rate liability wanted to limit its outflows should interest rates rise substantially and was willing to give up some potential gains should there instead be a dramatic decline in short-term rates. To achieve this end the firm could modify a simple interest rate swap contract to read as follows: As long as the interest rate neither rises by 200 basis points nor falls more than 100 basis points, the firm pays a floating rate and receives a fixed rate; but, if the interest is more than 200 basis points above or 100 basis points below the current rate, the firm receives and pays a fixed rate. The resulting payoff profile for this floating floor-ceiling swap is illustrated in Panel A of Figure 5.

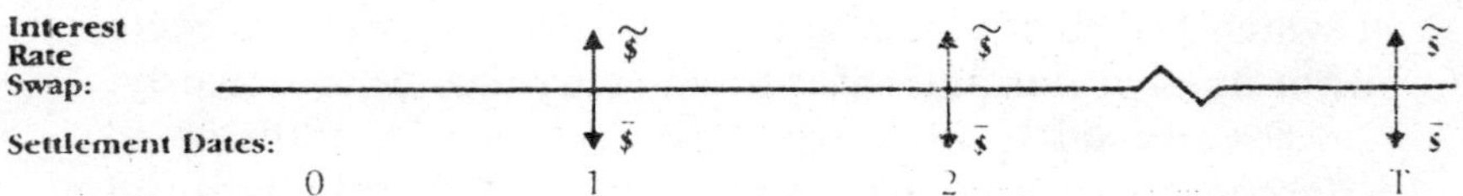

Fig. 3 : Cash Flows in an Interest Rate swap
The firm illustrated pa· s a fixed dollar interest rate ($) and receives interest computed on a floating dollar rate ($). The counterpart · pa· s floating and receives fixed.

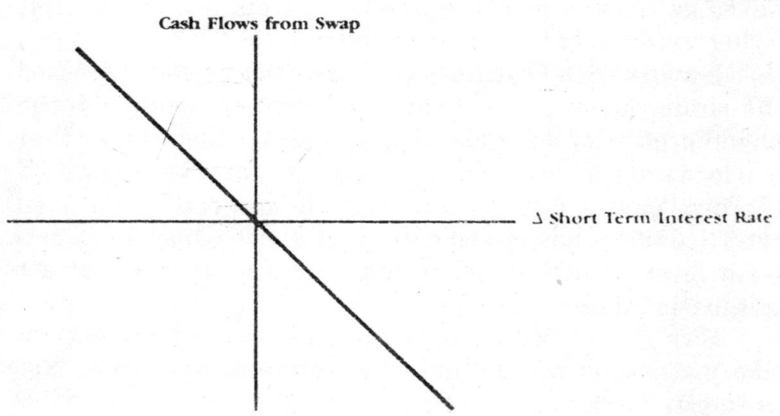

Fig. 4 : Pa· off Profile of an Interest Rate Swap for Firm Pa· ing Floating Rate and Receiving Fixed Rate

Panel A: Floating Floor-Ceiling Swap

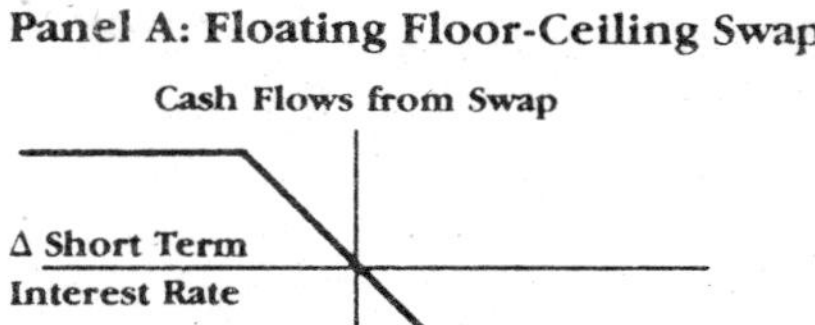

Panel B: Fixed Floor-Ceiling Swap

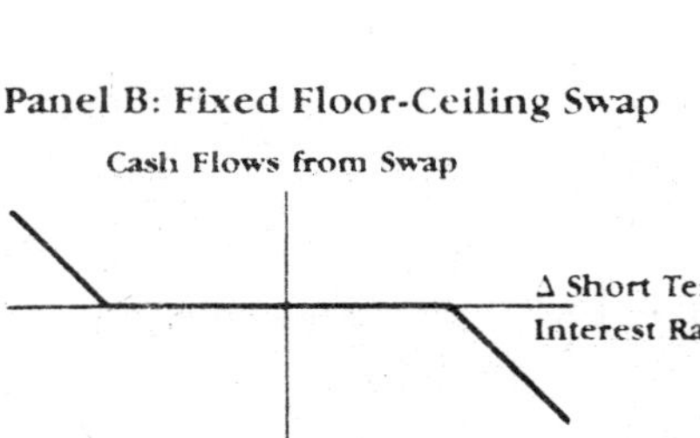

Fig. 5 : Pa· -off Profile for Floor-Ceiling Swaps
Firm receives a fixed rate and pays a floating rate between the limits set by the floor and ceiling rates.
Firm receives a fixed rate and pays a fixed rate between the limits set by the floor and ceiling rates.

Conversely, the contract could have been modified as follows: As long as the interest rate is within 200 basis points of the current rate, the firm receives and pays a fixed rate; but if the interest rate rises or falls by more than 200 basis points, the firm pays a floating rate and receives a fixed rate. The payoff profile for the resulting fixed floor-ceiling swap is illustrated in panel B of Figure 5.

Given the range of swaps described above, we agree with the market participant who noted that "the future potential structures... .are limited only by the imagination and ingenuity of those participating in the market."

Development of the Swaps Market

The swaps market is still relatively new. As we noted, its origins can be traced to the parallel loan products of the 1970s. However, a market for swaps did not exist in any meaningful sense until the 1980s. Currency swaps are slightly older than interest rate swaps; their public introduction was the World Bank-IBM transaction in August 1981. US dollar-denominated interest rate swaps started in 1982. While not as old as the currency swaps market, the US interest rate swaps market is now the largest of the swaps markets.

Given the growth in swaps that has occurred, there are two questions we want to consider in this section: (1) Since swaps are so similar to forward contracts, WHY did this market evolve? (2) In order to provide a framework for looking at the future of this market, what path has the evolution of this market followed so far—HOW did this market evolve?

Why Did the Swaps Market Evolve?

Trade journals and market participants agree that the growth of the swaps market has resulted from the ability to receive "significant cost savings" by combining a bond issue with a swap. Using swaps, the firm ends up with lower borrowing costs than it could have obtained with a single transaction. For example, with the use of swaps, companies have obtained funding at LIBOR minus 75-100 basis points. Obviously, a satisfying explanation of why the swaps market evolved must identify the source of this cost saving.

Financial Arbitrage : The popular argument seems to be that the cost savings is based on some kind of financial arbitrage across different capital markets. That is, prices in various world capital markets are not mutually consistent; and firms can lower their borrowing costs by going to foreign capital markets with lower rates, borrowing there, and then swapping their exposure back into their domestic currency, thereby ending with cheaper funding than that obtainable from simply borrowing at home.

The problem with this argument, however, is that the very process of exploiting this kind of opportunity should soon eliminate it. The opening and expansion of a swap market effectively increases the demand for loans in low-rate markets and reduces the demand in higher-rate markets, thereby eliminating the supposed rate differences. Moreover, if this were the only economic basis for swaps, the benefits to one party would come at the expense of the other. Thus, in reasonably efficient and integrated world capital markets, it seems difficult to attribute the continuing growth of the swaps market simply to interest rate differences, and thus financial arbitrage, among world capital markets.

Tax and Regulatory Arbitrage : Swaps allow companies to engage in what might be termed tax and regulatory arbitrage. Prior to the existence of a well-functioning swap market, a firm issuing dollar-denominated, fixed-rate bonds generally did so in US capital markets and thus had to comply with US securities regulation. Moreover, the issuing firm, as well as the security purchasers, were generally faced with the provisions of the US tax code. The introduction of the swap market allows an "unbundling," in effect, of currency and interest rate exposure from the regulation and tax rules in some very creative ways. For example, with the introduction of swaps, a US firm could issue a yen-denominated issue in the Eurobond market, structure the issue so as to receive favourable tax treatment under the Japanese tax code, avoid much of the US securities regulation, and yet still manage its currency exposure by swapping the transaction back into dollars. Unlike the classic financial arbitrage described above, there is no reason for opportunities for tax or regulatory arbitrage to disappear (barring changes, of course, in the various tax and regulatory codes).

To illustrate the manner in which tax and regulatory arbitrage induces swaps, consider the way one US firm used swaps to take advantage of special tax and regulatory conditions in Japan:

(1) Until recently, zero coupon bonds received extremely favourable treatment under the Japanese tax code: taxes were not due until maturity, and at maturity the difference between the purchase price and the face value of the bond was taxed at the capital gains rate.

(2) The Ministry of Finance limited the amount a pension fund could invest in non-yen-denominated bonds issued by foreign corporations to at most 10% of their portfolio.

In response to these conditions, a US firm issued a zero coupon yen bond plus a dual currency bond with interest payments in yen and principal repayment in dollars. The zero coupon yen bond permitted the firm to take advantage of the tax treatment of yen zeros. The Ministry of Finance ruled that the dual currency bonds qualified as ayen issue for purposes of the 10% rule, even though the dual currency bond has embedded within it a dollar-denominated zero. Hence, by issuing the dual currency bond, the US firm was able to capitalize on the desire of Japanese pension funds to diversify their portfolios internationally, while at the same time adhering to the regulation imposed by the Ministry of Finance.

The same US firm also, however, wanted to transform its resulting yen exposure to a US dollar exposure. To transform the bond issues, the firm used a currency swap together with a spot $/Y transaction. (There is less liquidity in non-standard, annuity-type swaps. By combining the principal repayment of the yen zero with the coupon payments of the dual currency bond, a standard, bond-type swap could be used to hedge.) The resulting cash flows are solely in dollars. Indeed, the swap transaction has created a synthetic deep discount dollar bond, and the rates were such that the firm lowered its total borrowing costs. By using the swap tran action, the firm capitalized on both the favourable regulatory ruling concerning dual currency bonds and the favourable tax treatment of zero coupon bonds, while retaining a fixed dollar interest rate exposure.

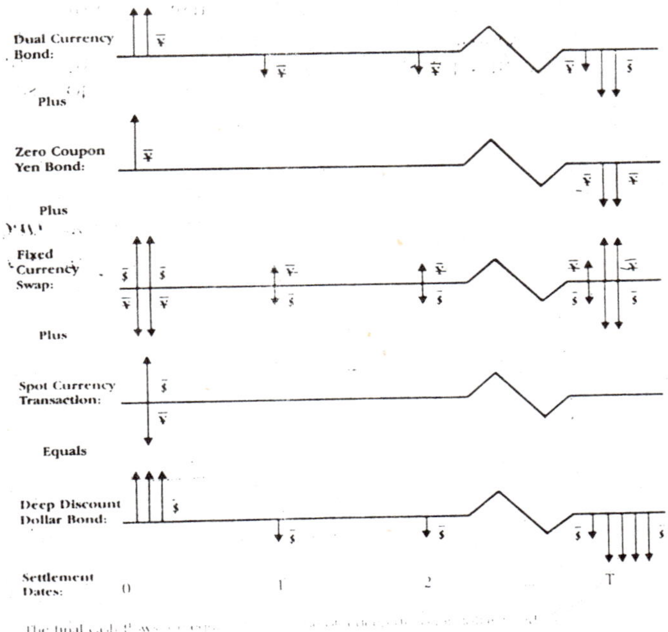

Fig. 6 : Cash Flows in a Dual Currenc · Bond Issue Plus a Zero Coupon Yen Issue Combined with a Fixed Currenc · Swap and Spot Currenc · Transaction.

Exposure Management : Swaps also allow firms to lower the transactions costs of managing their exposure to interest rates, currency prices, or commodity prices. As we noted, a fixed currency swap can be used by a firm to transform a debt incurred in pounds into a dollar liability. This transformation is illustrated in Figure 7. The payoff profile for a loan incurred in pounds relative to changes in the £/$ exchange rate is shown as the dashed line. The payoff profile for the swap is shown as the solid line. Viewed in this context, the swap contract behaves like a conventional long-dated foreign exchange forward contract; losses on the dollar-based loan resulting from exchange rate changes will be offset by gains on the swap contract.

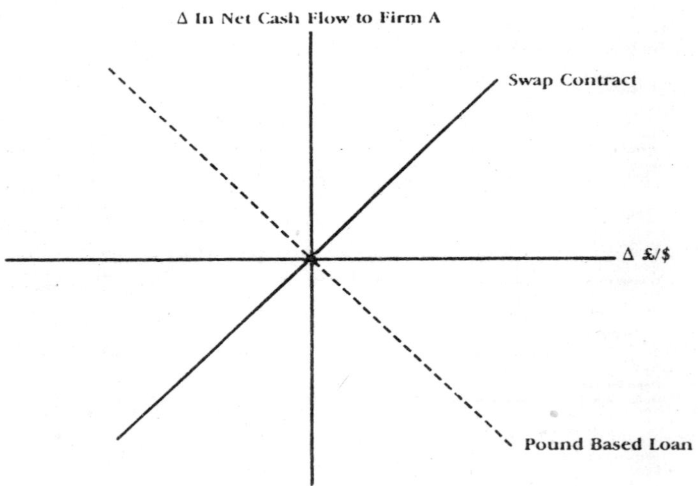

Fig. 7 : Pa· off Profile of a Currenc · Swap Used to Hedge the Financial Risk Exposure from its Underl· ing Business

The dashed line represents the exposure of the firm's net cash flow to changes in the £/$ exchange rate without hedging. The payoff profile for the swap is the solid line. Thus, after the swap, the firm is completely hedged against changes in this exchange rate.

For example, consider the case of a firm just entering a foreign market. Although well-known at home, the company might have difficulty placing debt in the foreign credit market where access to information about the firm is more expensive. In this case, it might be less expensive to issue debt in domestic capital markets and swap into the foreign currency exposure.

Conversely, suppose a firm's cash flow exposure in Deutschemarks declines, reducing the amount of DM-denominated debt desired in the firm's balance sheet. Without swaps, the firm would have to call outstanding DM bonds to manage its exposure, an expensive alternative if German interest rates have risen. With access to a liquid swap market, the firm may have a lower-cost means of reducing its DM-denominated liabilities.

Completing Markets : Finally, the swaps market contributes to the integration of financial markets by allowing market participants to fill gaps left by missing markets. An obvious gap filled by the swaps market is the forward market in interest rates. Until recently, there were no forward interest rate contracts available. But, because an interest rate swap behaves like a series of forward contracts, a swap could be used in place of the missing forward contract. Hence, the swap market can be used as a way of synthetically 'completing" the financial markets.

Less obvious is the manner in which currency and interest rates swaps have been used to fill gaps in the international financial markets. For example, there is no Swiss Treasury Bill market. Currency and interest rate swaps, however, can be used to create this market synthetically.

In sum, there are four primary reasons WHY the swaps market evolved: (1) classic financial arbitrage opportunities; (2) profit opportunities from regulatory and tax arbitrage; (3) lower transaction costs for some types of financial risk exposure management; and (4) financial market integration. It appears that the first of these is significantly less important today than when swaps markets first opened. Spreads which were initially available have been substantially reduced by the very process of financial arbitrage which produced the original cost savings. As one market observer has commented,

> *"....at the outset of the market, a 'AAA' issuer could reasonably expect to achieve 75-100 basis points below LIBOR on a bond/swap; under current conditions, this same issuer might expect*

only 25-30 basis points below. ..Many issuers now find it more cost-effective to approach the floating rate note market than the bond/swap market."

But if the opportunities for classic financial arbitrage have been eroded by competition, the other three factors remain important and can be expected to stimulate further activity in swaps.

How Did the Swaps Market Evolve?

A picture of the historical development of the swaps market can be obtained by looking either at the evolution of the products or at changes in the market's participants. Both tell the same story. We first look at the products.

As we noted, currency swaps were the first to appear. The earliest swaps were done on a one-off basis, which involved a search for matching counter-parties—matching not only in the currencies, but also in the principal amounts desired. These early swaps were custom-tailored products. Because the deals were all one-off, they involved a great deal of work by the financial institution arranging the swap; but—and this is a crucial point—they involved virtually no direct exposure for the intermediary. In the language of the market participants, the early swaps required "creative problem solving" rather than capital commitment from the intermediary.

As interest rate swaps began to appear, the movement toward a more standardized product began. With the US dollar interest rate swaps, there were fewer areas in which counterparties might not match than had been the case for currency swaps. The product had become more homogeneous; and because the product had become more homogeneous, there was less demand for one-off deals. Instead of requiring an exactly matching counterparty, the intermediary could bundle counterparties.

With the move toward homogeneity and the reduced reliance on an identifiable counterparty, markets for swaps—in particular, interest rate swaps—began to look more and more like markets for commodities. Increased competition forced down the spreads. And, with the increased competition, an extensive search for a counterparty or group of counterparties was unprofitable for the intermediary. Instead, the intermediaries began to accept swap contracts without a counterparty, taking the risk into their own books and either matching it internally with an offsetting position or hedging it with government securities or instruments in the financial futures market.

Hence, the evolution of the products offered in the swaps market paralleled that of most markets; swaps evolved from a customized, client-specific product to a standardized product. With the customized product, the role of the intermediary had been one of problem solving. As the product became more standardized, the role of the intermediary changed considerably, with less emphasis on arranging the deal and more on transactional efficiency and capital commitment.

Looking at the participants in the swaps market, the dominant intermediaries in the early stage of development were investment banks. As the market evolved, the entrants into this market were more highly capitalized firms, in particular commercial banks. This evolution fits precisely with that of the products. In the early stages the emphasis was on the intermediary arranging the transaction rather than accepting risk from the transaction; thus investment banks were the natural intermediaries. But, as the swaps became more standardized, it became essential for the intermediary to be willing and able to accept part or all of a potential transaction into its books. Hence commercial banks, with their greater capitalization, became a more significant factor.

As we noted, the path the swaps market followed in its evolution is similar to that other markets have taken—most notably, the development of the options market. Prior to 1973, the market for put and call options in the U.S. was an over-the-counter market. Members of the Put and Call Dealer's Association would write options, but only on a one-off basis. Each option was virtually unique because (1) the maturity date was set 181 days from the date the contract was written and (2) the exercise price was set as a function of the prevailing stock price (usually at the stock price). The result was that, for options, there was little volume, little liquidity, and virtually no secondary market. The growth of the options market occurred after the Chicago Board Options Exchange standardized the contracts (maturity dates and exercise prices) and developed an active secondary market. Dealing with a homogeneous product rather than individual customized deals, market makers were able to manage their risks by managing bid-ask spreads to maintain a neutral exposure rather than hedging each transaction on a one-off basis. While over-the-counter options are still offered, the real liquidity in the options market is in exchange-listed options. The options market evolved by moving from an individualized, custom-made product to one resembling a commodity.

While swaps have not evolved to the point of becoming exchange-traded instruments (a point to which we will return in our final section), the paths of evolution—particularly the major factors—have been similar. As was the case with options, contract standardization has played a major role. One market observer put it well by noting that "swaps have become a high volume, lower margin business, rather than the personalized, corporate financial deal of the past." As we have pointed out, the standardization has been more pronounced for interest rate swaps, which may go a long way in explaining why this market has grown more rapidly than that for currency swaps.

Also paralleling the development of options markets, the growth of the swap market corresponded to the liquidity available through the secondary market. While positions can be traded, the secondary market in swaps normally involves the reversing (unwinding) of a position. The simplest method to unwind a swap would involve a cancellation of the agreement, with a final difference check determined on the basis of the remaining value of the contract. However, since this simple "unwind" could result in taxable income, the more common method of unwinding a swap is by writing a "mirror" swap to cancel out the original. Most market observers indicate that this market is sufficiently deep to decrease risks in the primary market, particularly for short-term swaps. Indeed, a 24-hour market now exists for dollar interest rate swaps of up to 12-year maturities and amounts to $500 million.

Pricing Swaps

The pricing of a swap transaction is the aspect of the swap market that has received the most attention, especially that part of pricing which concerns credit risk. The pricing of a swap involves more, however, than just that single dimension. In fact swap pricing can be viewed as having three major components : forward prices, transaction costs, and the credit risk inherent in the transaction.

Forward Prices : Central to any swap agreement is the forward price—whether it be the forward interest rate, the forward exchange rate, or the forward price of a commodity—embodied in the exchange. Earlier we demonstrated that a swap contract is fundamentally a series of forward 8 In this view, the forward rate embodied in a swap contract must be the same as the forward rates employed in other corresponding financial contracts such as bonds and futures. And the empirical evidence bears this out: the difference between the two year swap rate and the forward rate implied by Eurodollar futures declined from over 50 basis points in 1982 and 1983 to less than 20 basis points in 1984; the remaining 20 basis points essentially reflect the difference in transaction costs and credit risk. This development also confirms our expectation that once the initial financial arbitrage opportunities discussed earlier are exhausted, the forward rates for swaps must conform to the market's view of the future as reflected in the prevailing term structure.

The forward rate component of the pricing of a swap, then, is determined neither by the intermediary nor by the swap market. It is determined by competition from other credit market instruments. Because a swap is a package of forward contracts, the forward rates reflected in the swap must conform to the market's view of the forward rate, or financial arbitrage will be profitable.

Transaction Costs : This component would be reflected in the bid/ask spread for a risk-free transaction plus any origination fees that are charged.9 The primary determinant of the bid/ask spread is the demand for liquidity. Put another way, the bid/ask spread is determined not by the market maker but, like the forward rate component, by competition in the market. The bid-ask spread, in short, is a market-determined price which reflects the costs of market-making activities.

Credit Risk : In contrast to the preceding components, both of which are independent of the counterparties, the credit risk premium is determined by the specific credit risk of the intermediary and/or the counterparties. The premium added to the bid/ask spread to reflect nonperformance risk depends on characteristics of the counterparty and of the intermediary arranging the swap; it must therefore reflect an appropriate compensation for the probability of default.

It has been argued by some observers that credit risk in a swap contract is priced "too low" relative to the pricing of credit risk in the loan market. To attempt to evaluate such a statement, we examine the determinants of the credit risk premium.

In a loan, the lender has at risk not only the obligated interest payments, but also the loan principil. In a swap the intermediary has at risk only the net cash flow difference at each settlement date. The difference in exposure implies that, for equal levels of nonperformance risk, the credit-risk premium associated with a swap would be far smaller than for a loan of comparable size.

As with a loan, the exposure of the intermediary issuing the swap contract to this firm—or, more precisely, its portfolio exposure to similar firms—is a determinant of the credit-risk premium. However, one element is significantly more important in the case of a swap contract. If the counterparty is arranging the swap as a hedge and if the counterparty has outstanding lines of credit with the intermediary, the swap decreases expected nonperformance losses of the loan. A counterparty which uses a swap to hedge its financial exposure is reducing its overall probability of financial distress. The probability of default for a swap, and therefore the risk premium, depend critically on whether or not the swap has been arranged as a hedge.

Consider the situation in which the swap is a hedge. During periods when the firm would be in financial distress, the swap contract would be in the firm's favour; the firm would be receiving difference checks. For example, consider a firm that experiences some financial difficulty if short-term interest rates rise. Suppose that this firm has entered into an interest rate swap to hedge its interest rate exposure. When short-term interest rates rise, the firm does indeed experience a decline in operating cash flow from its core business; but, at the same time, the firm is receiving inflows from the swap contract. In such a situation, even a firm in financial distress would have no incentive to default on the swap contract.

Therefore, if the swap is a hedge, the probability of default on the swap contract, as well as the probability of default on other liabilities such as loan contracts, are both reduced by this active financial risk exposure management; and the credit risk premiums attached to swap contracts should reflect this difference.

By contrast, if the swap had been used *not* to create a hedge, but rather to speculate on movements in financial markets, the probability of default on the swap is higher and the risk premium shoul be correspondingly greater. In the same way, if the swap is acting as a reverse hedge, the swap would increase the intermediary's exposure.

The above argument suggests that the credit risk assigned to a swap contract should not be based solely on a credit review of the counterparty. The credit risk associated with a swap contract depends on the exposure of the intermediary to firms similar to the one seeking a swap contract and on whether or not the swap acts as a hedge.

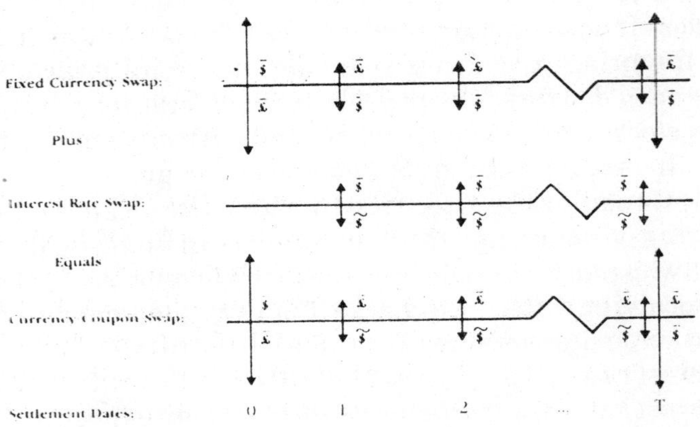

Fig. 8 : A Currenc · Coupon Swap from Fixed-Rate Pounds to Floating-Rate Dollars Viewed as a Combination of a Fixed Currenc · Swap from Pounds to · ears Plus an Interest Rate Swap from Fixed-Rate Dollars to Floating-Rate Dollars

We have purposely not dealt with more technical aspects of credit risk, such as the degree to which risks change if a swap is unwound, the credit risk implications of trading swap positions, and the legal standing of swap contracts in a bankruptcy. (Some of these will be considered in the next section.) Instead, our objective has been to point out what we think are the special features in evaluating the credit risk of a swap: (1) there is no principal at risk so we have "settlement risk" rather than "credit risk" per se; and (2) whether the swap is used as a hedge is an important factor. On the basis of what we have seen, we tend to be more optimistic than many observers about the probability of defaults. One piece of evidence consistent with our view is the fact that in June of 1985, Citicorp determined that it had been overcautious, and thus reduced its assessment of credit risk, in its pricing of swaps.

Pricing Restrictions from Arbitrage : Our major emphasis has been on viewing swaps as packages of forward contracts. We believe that the approach of pricing swaps by breaking them down into a set of fundamental cash flows is by far the most general, and thus the least restrictive, framework for evaluating new products; it is also likely to be the most flexible in solving pricing problems for very tailored swaps. At the same time, however, we have suggested that complicated swaps can also be decomposed into more simple swaps. For example, as Figure 8 demonstrates, a currency coupon swap is equivalent to a fixed currency swap plus a simple interest rate swap. The idea of unbundling swaps into other swaps can be important in identifying arbitrage opportunities within the market. For example, the cost of a currency coupon swap should be compared to the cost of a simple interest rate swap plus a fixed currency swap. Because they are equivalent transactions, the sum of the prices of the least costly alternative for each component is the best guide to pricing the complex swap.

Moreover, from the perspective of the intermediary, swap decomposition is important for exposure management by the intermediary. Again considering a currency swap, it may be easier to find counterparties for a currency coupon swap by looking for separate counterparties for the interest rate and the currency swap components.

The Future of the Swap Market

We do not purport to be able to predict the future for this market. Indeed, we subscribe to the adage that "he who lives by the crystal ball ends up eating ground glass." Certain factors, however, are likely to have the largest impact on the future evolution of this market. In this section, we will point out those factors we think are most important and suggest possible outcomes.

Liability of the Intermediary : Much of what we

have read in the trade journals and heard from the market participants involves conjecture about the swap market "after the first major default." This reflects uncertainty about the legal standing of swap contracts and, more significant, a good deal of controversy over the liability borne by the intermediary. At one extreme, there are those who argue that the intermediary should assume no liability. Proponents of this view recommend making swaps more like exchange-traded instruments. Suggestions include marking swaps to market with callable margins and collateralization.

At the other extreme are those who argue that the intermediary should always retain part of the risk. Arguing against the move toward exchange trading, proponents of this position note that, because swaps are like bundles of forward contracts, credit risk of the counterparties is an important element; and the intermediary is effectively a counterparty to each side of the contract.

Secondary Market : As we noted, the growth of the secondary market has made possible much of the growth of the swaps market, and future growth depends on the existence of an active secondary market. Whether a still broader secondary market should be encouraged inevitably throws us back on the earlier question of the liability of the intermediary. Proponents of making swaps exchange-traded instruments point out that marking to market or collateralizing permit contract standardization as well as providing effective guarantees against contractual default. Furthermore, if contracts are effectively bonded, as would be the case with marking to market or collateralizing, the secondary markets can be more anonymous.

Opponents of the move toward exchange trading for swaps point out that secondary markets can be active even if the assets are not homogeneous. For example, there exists an active secondary market for mortgaged-backed securities. In this market, performance is guaranteed by mortgage insurance and the reputation of the originating institution. And it is argued that similar mechanisms are also possible in the swaps market.

Regulation : As might be expected, the divisions evident in the preceding issues are also evident when it comes to questions concerning appropriate regulation of this market. One group argues that additional contractual guarantees are necessary if abuses in this market are to be avoided. Hence, in this view, regulation should take the form of codifying the contractual guarantees—for example, requiring that the contracts be marked to market or collateralized. Those taking the opposite position argue that this market is an simply an extension of credit markets and that imposing liability on the financial intermediary is the best way to limit potential abuses.

Besides this controversy over how to regulate, there is also the issue of who should regulate swaps. There are differences in regulatory bodies across countries, and also multiple regulatory bodies within the same country, that need to be considered. Under such circumstances, effective regulation will be difficult if not impossible because it requires coordination both within and among countries. If the US, for example, decided to place burdensome regulations on swaps, the principal effect on swap activity would be to change the location of swap transactions. Even if a group of the major countries acted in concert, the economic incentives for swaps discussed earlier suggest that there would be strong motive for some country to supply a favourable legal environment.

The future of the swaps market, then, appears to turn on whether that market moves further in the direction of becoming a widely-traded exchange. While we are not comfortable in predicting the direction the market will actually take, we are confident that the future composition of this market, both the users and the intermediaries, will depend strongly on the resolution of the above uncertainty. If swaps move further toward exchange trading, investment banks will be the major beneficiary. Removing the liability for the intermediary by marking to market or collateralizing would diminish the emphasis on capital commitment; and if so, investment banks might well regain the dominance they enjoyed in the earliest stages in the evolution of this market. On the other hand, if the intermediary continues to bear risk (or if the liability for the intermediary is increased), commercial banks will be the beneficiary.

The degree to which the swap market moves toward exchange trading will also determine the users of this market. With credit risk borne by the intermediaries, entry to the swaps market may well be denied to lesser credits. Hence, the predominant users of swaps will be the best credit risks. If the swaps market moves toward exchange trading, however, this composition will change. Lesser credit risks will be able to enter the swap market. Furthermore, to the extent that collateralization or some other form of bonding raises the cost of a swap transaction, the best credits will be expected to exit the market, refusing to pay the implicit insurance premium.

Because of the considerable dispute about the appropriateness of moving further toward exchange trading, there is no consensus about the future form of the swaps market. But there are issues where a consensus is possible. Most observers agree, for example, that while the market will continue to develop a more homogeneous set of products with greater liquidity, there will continue to exist a subset of swaps which are custom-tailored. The commercial banks should dominate in the homogeneous swaps market, which will be characterized by high volume, low spreads, and a significant capital commitment. Investment banks should continue to have a comparative advantage in the customized end of the market.

□□□

Index

❑❑❑